Praise for _Lig_

Though many in the media and the academ ... modern world, Lauren Green astutely observes that the heartfelt question, "Where is God in my hour of need?" is universal. In more than forty years of travel I have heard this plea countless times, whether from students in university forums or corporate leaders in private conversations. A seasoned journalist and an accomplished pianist, Lauren interviews scholars and discloses her own journey to understand God as a living reality. She has lived out her faith with courage and grace in a difficult arena. Her words will encourage and challenge you.

—Ravi Zacharias
Author and Speaker

This story of Lauren Green's spiritual journey, powerfully narrated and illustrated with moving stories of struggle and perseverance, will cast light up many blind alleys.

—George Weigel
Distinguished Senior Fellows, Ethics and Public Policy
Center, Washington, D.C.

I have known Lauren Green since she played piano on my old Fox News show _After Hours_. Her discovery of who God is and what it means to be loved and find meaning in a relationship with him will help the reader find meaning and purpose in his or her own life. Isn't that what we all seek?

—Cal Thomas
Syndicated Columnist

Lauren Green is one of the bright lights in American journalism, and she has distinguished herself as an astute analyst of religion and culture. _Lighthouse Faith_ is her new book, and, in it, she brings fresh insights and perspectives that readers will not have heard anywhere else! Her voice is thoroughly original, solidly biblical, and consistently inspiring. Having personally interviewed the world's leading figures in religion, plus drawing from her own knowledge of history and current events, Green introduces timeless truths in fresh new ways. Her explanation of how music theory relates to God (specifically as used by G. F. Handel) is absolutely riveting. In _Lighthouse Faith_ Lauren Green brings readers content that truly is unique.

—Alex McFarland
Director of The Center for Apologetics & Christian Worldview,
North Greenville University

LIGHTHOUSE FAITH

LIGHTHOUSE FAITH

God As a Living Reality in a World Immersed in Fog

LAUREN GREEN

W PUBLISHING GROUP

AN IMPRINT OF THOMAS NELSON

Lighthouse Faith

Published in Nashville, Tennessee, by W Publishing, an imprint of Thomas Nelson.

Thomas Nelson titles may be purchased in bulk for educational, business, fund-raising, or sales promotional use. For information, please email SpecialMarkets@ThomasNelson.com.

ISBN 978-0-7180-8340-3 (eBook)
ISBN 978-0-7180-8352-6 (HC)
ISBN 978-1-4003-4164-1 (TP)

Library of Congress Control Number: 2016917860

I dedicate this book to all of my family including, my mom Bessie Green, sisters Barbara Panser and Lois Porter, and brother Leslie R. Green. I especially want to dedicate this work to the family members who are no longer with us. To my father, Robert F. Green, for his tireless devotion to his family. To my brother Kenneth C. Green who, as he was dying of cancer, encouraged me to finish this project. And, of course, to my Great Aunt Wreatha, a simple Christian, whose incredible faith influenced me and helped mold the themes of these pages.

Your word is a lamp for my feet,
a light on my path.

PSALM 119:105

Contents

INTRODUCTION

Eye-opening Confessions

ONE OF MY MOST MEMORABLE ASSIGNMENTS AS A religion correspondent for Fox News was venturing into Times Square with cameraman in tow for what was supposed to be a lighthearted man-on-the-street segment, asking people how many of the Ten Commandments they had recently violated. The cornucopia of characters in the crossroads of the world always yields "great sound," as we say in the business.

While the final, edited version of this mission was rather humorous, the process was not. It really shed light on the somber state of the human heart—mine included. There were some embarrassing moments, as people would confess their most intimate sins, such as an adulterous affair, cheating a business partner, or even attempted murder. I wasn't equipped to handle such mea culpa. Searching for an explanation, I finally remembered something a wise minister once said that seemed to make sense of it all. He maintained that our most longed-for desire is first to be loved and then to be known and that the two—knowing and loving—cannot be separated. You cannot truly be loved unless you are truly known. But to be truly known requires that you make yourself vulnerable, no false masks, no cover-ups, just your soul laid bare. That's the only reason I could come up with as to why people would confess their sins to me, a stranger, and do it on camera for the world to see, no less. It was as if we, all of us, share some collective conscience that cries out to be liberated from the burden of trying to control our lives, trying to get ahead; the struggle to make something of ourselves and prove ourselves worthy or at least better at something than everyone else. To unshackle ourselves from what prevents us from being the people we were truly meant to be.

Not only did the question really test people's knowledge of God's holy laws, which was pretty dismal, but it also exposed how quickly people would open up about their indiscretions when confronted with a list of the commandments. It reminded me of that verse from Romans that says, "Every knee shall bow . . . every tongue shall confess to God" (14:11 NKJV). It also showed that knowledge changes everything, especially knowledge about God; for to love God means knowing that God and the Decalogue (the Ten Commandments) reveals a great deal about God and his world, and the way things work, but more on that later.

The escapade helped me see me something quite profound and powerful about the nature of divine law: it is intimately connected to divine love, and tied to it in a way that would shake the foundation of my world and completely alter the way I would view the entire created order, not to mention how I viewed my own dreams of contentment and fulfillment.

You see, my Times Square adventure was a humble eye-opener to my own shortfalls . . . because I, too, had once been confronted with a probing question that exposed my many faults and fig leaves. The question caught me off guard and struck the very core of what I lacked, knowledge about God. It unearthed the heart of what I craved, to feel loved by that same God. It was my pastor, best-selling author Dr. Timothy Keller, who asked the question, "Is God a concept to you, or is He a living reality?" In other words, he asked if God was more like an accessory, a handbag, a designer outfit, or an iTunes account, whose purpose was to serve me. More probing an angle, was God an array of spiritual ideas and philosophies strung together to fill the void of organized religion, to essentially affirm my life choices? Or, was God and his authoritative Word in the Bible an objective reality to which I daily shaped my life?

Being honest with myself, I had to admit that the former was more applicable. God was the good uncle, the adored grandpa who gave me what I wanted when I asked, and if he didn't, I was the petulant child, angry at being refused. But I knew that my heartfelt need was for the latter, to have God front and center. And I knew from the Times Square experience that once again, knowledge about God's holy laws just might be the key that could change everything.

This book is an extension of my relationship with Dr. Keller's pastoral challenge. It's a guide to discover *how* to experience God in my everyday life—how to respond to the real God versus creating my own version of the deity, but in a way that matches the reality of how the world we live in works, its consistency and order, its joys and sorrows, its struggles and victories. As we'll discover together, all of life and the wonder of the universe begin to make sense when we understand how and why God's laws are present. Just as a building will eventually crumble if it isn't built using precise mathematical laws, so will our lives and relationships fall apart if the right laws are not acknowledged. This is not God issuing some moralistic approach to life. It is his loving grace to show us that there is a path to what we desire, but we have to know which way to walk. I live in New York, and there is no way that I'm reaching Canada if I walk south. This is both a reality and a law that is unaffected by how much I pray or who I talk to about it. If I walk south, it's not happening. It is the same way with God's law. Just as he established through the cosmos and the principles of physics in the wider world, there are also ways that my own life will work. Ignoring those laws does not make me independent and powerful, it merely sets me up for failure. I am writing this book to help you see and accept this reality and to then be astounded, as I was, by just how much God's law permeates everything around us. It's incredibly beautiful, and by seeing it, you will understand his love more fully than ever before. He will become that living reality you seek.

One of the greatest lessons I learned about God was not from a scholar or a professor, but from a simple Christian, my great-aunt Wreatha. She is long past now, but left an indelible mark on the fabric of my life that I only now as an adult appreciate. She was a devout woman who taught Sunday school and was active in the church. Aunt Wreatha had no children of her own, but she influenced many through the years as a schoolteacher, educating several generations of young, impressionable minds. She would tell us stories about the teachers' college where she learned her craft and about the rural schoolhouse where she instructed poor children and uncomplicated country folk.

My sister Lois and I would often visit Aunt Wreatha and her husband, my Uncle Max, whom both of us feared a bit. As I think back on those days, I believe he just didn't like children too much. Uncle Max was as gruff and curt as Aunt Wreatha was patient and giving. By the time we came along, as the two youngest of five, they were retired and living in a small walk-up. So Aunt Wreatha played a game with us called Bunkum. It was a simple game two little girls could play without destroying their small apartment. Aunt Wreatha would take a common object, like a comb or a pair of scissors, and hide it in plain sight while we were out of the room. We'd then return to the room and look for the item. Despite being "hidden" in a visible spot—like laying vertical in a lampshade or peeking out from a crevice of the couch— the item sometimes took quite a while to find. But when one of us did find it, that person would say, "Bunkum," then sit down while the other one continued to search. It was a game we enjoyed so much that each of us took turns hiding the common object, then laughing in glee as the other players searched for and had trouble finding it.

It was in this game that Aunt Wreatha helped explain, perhaps unknowingly, a fundamental truth about the Almighty. You see, I get the feeling that God, through the last couple of millennia, has been playing a sort of cosmic game of Bunkum with us all. He's been hiding in plain sight. Just as a forest hides a tree or an ocean conceals drops of water. God is so big and so small at the same time that he's easy to overlook. One could travel the universe and never meet God, but then one day see him in all his glory in a single rose petal. When we are open to receiving him, God can touch our hearts in the simplest yet most profound ways. And so it was for me, with the game of Bunkum.

You might wonder, as many people do, why would God not make his presence obvious or give us empirical evidence of his existence? Why the game playing? I believe it has to do with his nature of pure love. He will not impose himself on us. We must choose to love him by our own free will.

There have been many "Bunkums!" shouted by millions of believing souls throughout the centuries. Many theologians and great men and women of faith have strengthened the beliefs of countless hearts and minds. But sometimes, in order for God to be a reality to us, to speak to us, we each need to find God in our own way. To meet God on the pathways of our own life's journey.

In that way, Bunkum has several lessons to teach all of us about God and about this world he has created. First, we shouldn't make God in our own image. The "hidden" object doesn't change form so that we can find it more easily. The players all search for the exact same object. We live in a world where individualism and finding your heart's desire is highly praised and valued. In a culture such as this, the natural tendency is to imagine a God who would be most like us and our experiences. For instance, we may believe in a judgmental god if we grew up in an authoritarian household. Or, if we grew up without boundaries, perhaps we believe in a permissive god, who accepts and forgives everybody's actions no matter what he or she has done. Or maybe, if we've endured a lot of hardships, we believe in an incompetent or uncaring god, one who's powerless or unwilling to end all the pain and suffering in the world.

Bunkum demands that regardless of your experiences and individuality, God is the same as he has always been. It is we who must change in our method of pursuit, perhaps only asking the God of the universe to reveal himself to us. It can be that simple. So often we try to fit God in a box, making God be what we want him to be. That can bring a lot of frustrations. But letting God be God can be incredibly freeing.

The second lesson to be learned from Bunkum is perseverance. All participants in the challenge of Bunkum never stopped searching until the hidden object was found. Sometimes it was found quickly, other times it took quite a while to locate. And when the search was challenging, every section, corner, and part of the room's landscape was thoroughly combed. We knew the object was there. We couldn't stop until it was found. But more important, we didn't want to stop. And so it is with our pursuit of God. Never stop. Never tire. We need only to search in order to find. The amazing thing is that when we finally find God, we realize that it was God all along who was really pursuing us. Grace is so amazing in that way! "I once was lost, but now am found, was blind, but now I see."[1]

And the third lesson from Bunkum: surprise and joy! When we finally discovered the hidden object, our reactions were always the same. We said, "It was so obvious. I can't believe I didn't see it sooner!" And, "It was there, right before my eyes!" That's because believing something is there doesn't mean perceiving it and living as though it is a part of your reality.

Practically speaking, we can believe in God as an abstract concept, just as I can know an object is in the room, yet remains hidden. But until I locate its whereabouts, it cannot always change my life. It doesn't change the status of my participation in the game; I am still a seeker. This is the difference between knowing *about* God and having an *experience* of his presence in your life. Searching can be an intellectual pursuit, just as in Bunkum, but finding the object alters my perception of the entire room. It also alters my relationship with the object and the room. After finding the object, the couch is not just a couch. It's three feet from where the object was hidden. The lamp is more than a lamp. It's the southern boundary of where the object lay on the table. The room is now defined by its relationship to the hidden object. And so it is in the world. When the living God is a reality, our everyday lives are defined by that relationship.

Perhaps the key to experiencing God is simply to see him in a whole new light, the light of his love. Ironically, that *light* just might be his law. Normally we think of love and law as two opposite ways of being. Yet one does not exist without the other. Remember the Times Square story? When those being interviewed felt known, they became open to a discussion on law. And both love and law together may be the key to seeing God hiding in plain sight. So our journey together will begin with a long recognized symbol of light, one that is designed to bring hope, comfort, and safety:

a lighthouse. It is an iconic image through which God's first commandment, of having no other god before him, can be understood so clearly. It resembles the fire atop the mountain from which the Commandments were first proclaimed and where we can experience how God's creation illuminates one truth: that we live in the reality of God's world, not he in ours.

CHAPTER 1

The Lighthouse

Therefore glorify the LORD in the dawning light,
The name of the LORD God of Israel in the coastlands of the sea.

—ISAIAH 24:15 NKJV

I HAVE NO DOUBT THAT THERE ARE PLACES ON EARTH with spiritual powers. They are abodes of solace and security—places like churches, of course, but also bucolic settings of verdant meadows, quiet rivers, or majestic forests. These serene locales are "living witnesses to the reality of God."[1] But what may not be so obvious, is that *common* places also hold spiritual powers, made spiritually potent by what God chooses to reveal to us while we are there.

I have been in such a place. It was at my friend Cathy's summer home on Long Island, New York, the area known as the Hamptons. But her house is not one of those mega-mansions raved about in magazines and on entertainment shows, or one of the Gatsby-esque gilded estates of a long-lost era. It is simple, almost farmhouse-like, with a cottage on about an acre and a half. It's a property that has been in Cathy's family for several generations, before the narrow sixty-mile stretch of land between the waters of the Great

Peconic Bay and the Atlantic Ocean became the summer playground of choice for the famous and super rich. Cathy herself is an extension of her home. I cannot separate that house from her incredible spirit. She is one of the true women of faith whom I have met in my life.

Cathy attends Mass daily and prays continually for her family, friends (including myself), and acquaintances. Despite her own tragedies, she seems always in good spirits and confident of God's ability to answer prayer. Like my own mother, she is a widow who, on top of losing her husband, has also suffered the death of a grown son. But you would never know her inner pain, for she radiates joy.

I hadn't known Cathy long when she first invited me to her summer-house. We met through my work as a religion correspondent. At first I saw her as a great source for stories because she's a member of the much-maligned (thanks to Dan Brown's *The Da Vinci Code*) Catholic lay organization Opus Dei. *Opus Dei* means "the work of God," and the ministry is founded on the principle that everyday activities can be made holy if they are pursued to the glory of God. In other words, life itself, in all of its ups and downs, is a calling. Cathy certainly lived out that doctrine, teaching by example that serving God is not a nine-to-five job. It's a way of being. And so it didn't take long for this spiritual woman to sense my brokenness and great need.

I was at one of the lowest points of my life. There were so many changes and traumas that seemed overwhelming at the time. One of those changes was a transition from one position to another at Fox. Although I love my current work as a religion correspondent, I had previously also been the news cut-in anchor for a popular morning show, and it seemed like a demotion. The move was made more intense because of a recent failed relationship, leaving me no loving shoulder to lean on, no domestic stability, and no anchor of my own to keep my vessel steady.

I was a single woman supporting myself in one of the most expensive and competitive cities in the world. A disruption like that, not of my own choosing, was rattling to the point of earth shattering.

I have to admit that I don't handle change well. I felt trapped in a cruel world, abandoned by the God I had believed in all my life, as if the God I was devoted to was removing his blessing and instead was bringing me to a place of wilderness, then leaving me there to fend for myself.

So coming to Cathy's simple home was like coming to a sanctuary. I felt reborn and rejuvenated. Instead of coiled up like a fetus in my New York City apartment, I was able to stretch my limbs both physically and emotionally in the home's welcoming arms: its cozy fireplace radiated a sense of security; the stuffed sofa and chairs in the living room cushioned my contorted conscience, and the front porch where I'd sit staring at the lawn brought a solace I had long forgotten. Couple that with lots of family photos on the walls and the constant whir of conversation and cooking in the kitchen, and it restored in me the belief that my life had meaning and purpose, that relationships mattered immensely, and that one in particular was guiding me ever so lovingly and mercifully.

And it was in Cathy's home that I began to realize that God had not forgotten me after all. It was quite the opposite. In fact, he was blessing me. He had brought me to a place in my life to get my attention; first emotionally with turmoil, then physically with this sanctuary. What looked to me like adversity, calamity, and disaster was actually God looking beyond my faults and my wants, and seeing to my needs. Through Cathy, the grace of God shone bright. I knew it for certain because of one quiet moment when God spoke to me through something so ordinary and so common—the depth of relationship and the calming presence of his created world.

I return to Cathy's home often. In the years since that inaugural visit so much has changed. I've learned that I must wholly lean on God no matter the circumstances, a daily challenge. Then later, I became comfortable with the new position at Fox. And finally, I met a wonderful man to whom I am now married. We often stay at Cathy's place to get away from the city. But several times before we dated or even met, I would go there on my own or with my niece Nicole, just to be part of Cathy's big family gatherings.

Many times I would go there to write. The early-morning solitude and quiet opened the portholes of my mind, unburdening it of pettiness so that the God I serve could speak to me. It was on one of those times at Cathy's place that I happened to take notice of a small framed photo of a lighthouse. The photo had always been there, sitting on a dresser, but I'd never really taken study of it until that one quiet summer morning when God chose to reveal himself to me. There were no blaring trumpets or quaking revelations. Just an ordinary moment taking note of a photo. It's an old black-and-white, grainy image of gray skies and a white-washed brick lighthouse with tiny shacks nestled on either side. A white picket fence encircles the entire group of buildings. Although whoever built the tiny dwellings and fence may have thought to protect the lighthouse from would-be usurpers, the picture gives the impression that the structures are huddling close to the lighthouse for their own protection.

Lighthouses are like that, you know. Their mere presence has been an assured sign to both mariners and land dwellers throughout the ages that all is not lost, that there is hope for safe journeys. That tiny photo of a lighthouse was certainly a sign of hope for me. I had come through a storm, and in that moment of quietness, God showed me it was his light guiding the way, his omniscient care shepherding my steps. So I began to try to understand the attraction to these lighthouses, these sentinels of the sea.

What I quickly learned was that lighthouses were, for many years, deeply necessary, because the sea can be an unforgiving master, the rocky shores a tempestuous beast. Stated beautifully by a wonderful documentary called *America's Lighthouses*, "The lighthouse lamps provide a few visual aids for vessels plying treacherous waters."[2] Without lighthouses, those at sea would not only have been lost, but would also be in serious danger, or worse, suffer death.

That lighthouses also possess spiritual symbolism is no surprise; we all search for a ray of hope in life's darkest moments. And lighthouses are physical symbols of that and other spiritual truths, which we will explore in more detail.

Practically, of course, lighthouses are built of earthly materials. Stone, brick, glass, and iron are all arranged into high towers of varying heights. The early lanterns needed oil for power, which the lighthouse keeper would bring up the winding staircase several times a day.

And the lighthouse keepers are almost prophet-like, as immortalized in R. L. Stevenson's *The Light Keeper*,

The brilliant kernel of the night,
The flaming lightroom circles me:
I sit within a blaze of light
Held high above the dusky sea.[3]

The keepers' sacrifice and steadfast devotion can be almost savior-esque, like the ailing William Major Perry who died kneeling in prayer in the Killick Shoals Lighthouse in Chincoteague, Virginia, rather than abandon his post.

Unfortunately, in later years automated systems made lighthouse keepers obsolete. The human senses of eyes that see, ears that hear, and a heart that cares would no longer be needed for saving souls on open waters. Radar, GPS, and the vast assortment of technological gadgetry now help vessels navigate safely. But regardless of the science that's replaced the tower beacons, we cannot replace their poignant relevance.

Henry Osmer could tell you about that. He is the resident historian of the Montauk Lighthouse, which overlooks the waters on the far eastern tip of Long Island, New York. It's the large lamp sitting high on a bluff, illuminating the space where the Atlantic Ocean meets the Long Island Sound. Osmer can recite to any visitor, as he did to me, about its strategic spot where nearly two hundred fifty years ago, British troops camped and plotted against General George Washington's forces during the American Revolutionary War. He can tell you every detail about why, a few years later, *President* George Washington commissioned the building of the Montauk Point Light, knowing its importance to the country's commerce and trade.

However, Osmer, now well into his sixties, choked back tears when he recalled his first sight of the lighthouse, when his father brought him to the point back in the early 1950s.

"I was only seven years old," he said. "But you know the thing is, I can still remember what it was like to see that. I mean, I'd never seen a lighthouse before. And it just mesmerized me. Just, the way it looked . . . this tall tower. I didn't understand what it was for. But the amazing size of it, how it was standing up there so big and beautiful, it stuck with me."

Osmer isn't alone in his love of lighthouses.

Extreme fisherman and minister Matthew Buccheri shares those sentiments as well. He's a lighthouse enthusiast and the Montauk Lighthouse is one of his local favorites. I first knew Reverend Buccheri as one of the pastors at my church in New York City. I was always struck by how he looked more like an '80s rock star than a man of religion, with his spiked, jet-black hair, black garb, and one earring. But on top of being a "fisher of men" like the apostle Peter, Buccheri, as a hobby, angles for flounder or striped bass on the shores below the Montauk Lighthouse. When I spoke to him after service one Sunday, he told me he was writing a book about lighthouses, that they fascinated him. I told him, too, about my new writing project titled "The Lighthouse," and it seemed like fate that we should talk more. A few weeks later we met for lunch in a crowded Thai restaurant in New York's Lower East Side. Despite being surrounded by bustling city noises, Buccheri described with clarity the sights and sounds of the Montauk Lighthouse.

He told me, "Down underneath that light . . . and in the middle of the night in a fog . . . they have a horn that goes off at that light. 'Whooooooo!'" he said, mimicking loudly the fog sound, his tone never making any of the typical New Yorkers in the restaurant blink twice. "And you see the light, it comes around in the fog, you sort of feel secure. Even though you're not a boat, I'm just fishing, you know you're on solid ground."

Buccheri says lighthouses are just "fires on a stick." So simple a mechanism, and yet they create a powerful effect. "There's kind of an aura, when you're standing in a lighthouse," he pined. "And it's . . . it's almost like a life. It has a spirit. It almost wants to speak to you."

But what could it be saying?

THE DARK NIGHT OF THE SOUL

So, on a visit to Cathy's home, I returned to that snapshot of the lighthouse to further study this visage, to ponder and grasp more of its message.

And I noticed something that I had missed before in this simple archetypical emblem. Entwined in the feelings of comfort and strength, there was something more stirring. There was sorrow. It was easy to miss because, of course, there is comfort to those seeking security, and there is strength for those seeking a pathway home to safety after a tiring journey. But the sorrow, it was for those who could not or would not look to its beacon for help. It was the first time I realized that God, through his infinite love and power, had not only shown me his care like a dutiful parent leading me to safe passage, he had also felt my pain. He had cried *with* me. He had taken up the burden of my hardship and bore it as his own. He had not stood far off, shaking his finger, and saying, "Next time do better." He knew I had lost my way, trying to find solace, security, and salvation through my career and relationships. They had become my beacons of hope. But when those things were shaken, I felt like all those who lose their way, and sometimes their lives, when they could not find the light in the darkness. I felt that in my darkest hour I was living out those lyrics from a haunting song by Gordon Lightfoot: "Does anyone know where the love of God goes when the waves turn the minutes to hours?"[4]

It is a question that many of us have asked in our own way; the sentiment of "Where is God in my hour of need?" is universal. It speaks to the human condition that ponders existence, questioning whether there is a God at all, or at least one who cares. It harbors resentment and anger at that same God from whom comfort, salvation, and redemption are sought. These are the words of Thomas Aquinas's *Dark Night of the Soul*.

At the climax of life's most defining moments of tragedy, trauma, or loss, we look to something outside ourselves to bring us through the storm, to make sense of it all, and to give weight and purpose to the feeble few years we have on this earth. I had looked to earthly sources. But Lightfoot's words, perhaps unknowingly, point to an ultimate source of hope.

So it's not surprising that his profound ode was penned in response to one of the most mysterious shipwrecks of the twentieth century, the sinking of the *SS Edmund Fitzgerald*. For many years now I have been intrigued by the story of the *Fitzgerald* and its doomed voyage. Perhaps because I have never forgotten hearing the ballad on the radio as a teenager, or the shock of learning that it was the story of a real ship that sunk in what we Minnesotans would consider our backyard. The *Fitzgerald* went down in the icy, fresh waters of Lake Superior in 1975 during a particularly nasty and wicked storm, known to mariners as "The Witch of November." Twenty-nine sailors were aboard. All were lost. Those words from Lightfoot's mournful ballad describe the iron ore carrier's last remaining hours of life; not the technical readout of the ship's metal hull while being assaulted by stormy waters, but the heartfelt desires of every soul on board during those traumatic minutes.

They were hardworking men, none of them perfect, but all understood that life had its good and bad days. And where one couldn't say for sure if any of the men were armchair philosophers or Bible-thumping believers, we can be assured that, like most sailors who spend ample time on water, they understood they were not totally in charge of their lives. They knew there was an uncertainty to life adrift in a vessel not of their own making. They knew of forces outside of themselves demanding to be respected and heeded. An authority that dictated how fast they traveled, what routes were taken and when. To challenge it recklessly could bring destruction or even death. For "the waves and wind still know" their master's voice. And it is not man's; it is God's.[5]

And in a very real sense, we are all mariners on the sea of life, traveling in these fleshy vessels not of our own making. From heartbeats and hymn singing, to the joys and sorrows of jobs, family, and friends, life's many rhythms mimic the motion of the waves, its pulses drive us on toward a distant shore, to the home we long for, where there is perfect peace, perfect love, perfect happiness. We look for light in a darkened world to guide us.

THE LIGHT

Maybe that's why lighthouses hold such fascination for many; they strike at some fundamental need for a light in the darkness, for a source of salvation and hope. So it's worth taking a deeper look at light, the element that gives lighthouses their peculiar personality, and the characteristics of which are the first natural law that we'll explore together. While light's ubiquitous presence in our lives—as sunlight, moonlight, or the flip of a switch—is easy to take for granted, light itself is a most curious phenomenon and has been since the dawning of time.

Light is God's first stated act of creation. Genesis declares, "And God said, 'Let there be light'" (1:3). It sounds a great deal like the Big Bang when "a burst of radiant energy expanded dramatically outward from an infinitesimal point 13.7 billion years ago."[6]

Between these two accounts lay a plethora of definitions of *light*: as electromagnetic forces, the sun and fire, warmth and radiation; it is the first rays of dawn through a bedroom window; fireworks on the Fourth of July, the aurora borealis magnifying an arctic sky. It is shafts of brightness penetrating a dense forest, or a full moon's reflection on a winding river.

But it also includes light as a transparent object, floating and fleeting, a pale palette in shades of a favored color. But even still in its more ethereal quality, light also exists in forms of illumination of thought and knowledge that brings understanding.

In all these things, light is primarily *one* thing: a source outside of ourselves, which we need. And that is key. "Maybe light isn't really something we see, but something that we *need to* see,"[7] theologian and scientist Alister McGrath once told me in an interview. And mathematician John Lennox also said to me in one of our talks at Oxford, England, one spring morning, that quite simply, "Light is one of those things that has so many different levels. It's a fundamental concept."[8]

Both McGrath and Lennox are members of an emerging breed that I've come to know through research and work. They are scientists with a strong faith. And their faith is not in spite of their scientific knowledge, but a direct result of it. As they explained to me, the more they understand scientific laws, the more it points to a divine Law Giver. Like so many brilliant people, they are able to find profound insights in the simplest observations.

Lennox especially, with his impish grin and Irish brogue, adeptly opened the eyes of my mind to a whole new understanding of light. Just as in the game of Bunkum, it was always there hiding in plain sight. It only needed the proper lens, which Lennox provided. When I asked him to further explain to me this idea of light as "fundamental," instead of speaking platitudes, he posed a question, as all wise teachers do. He asked me, "Why did God create a universe in which human beings didn't have a built-in light?"[9] In other words, why can't we be our own lighthouses, able to see clearly in the dark?

Lennox pointed out to me that there are many creatures that are bioluminescent, equipped with their own light. Many sea creatures possess this kind of light, enabling them to see and be seen in the blackness of deep waters. Fireflies, too, twinkle in the dusk of a summer's eve, appearing as tiny, earthbound stars. Animals like owls, cats, and deer see in darkness, making their nocturnal wanderings almost mysterious to humans. Then there are creatures like bats that don't see at all but navigate using biological sonar.

Yet for all its complexity and supposed superiority, the human brain, which processes trillions of bits of information within seconds through more than one hundred billion neurons and synaptic pathways, cannot see in the dark without the aid of an outside source. We, who the Bible says are made in the image of God, are so utterly and completely dependent on outside light sources. It's a curious thing, as Lennox pointed out. Why would God make us that way? If he had made us bioluminescent, we would have no need for lighthouses. We would be our own source of light.

This is an important observation. Lennox is saying that God has placed physical light in front of us and separated it from us, as a testimony and living sermon, for us to understand what we would have never understood if we could see in darkness on our own: that we need knowledge of *him* to see and function properly. That is how we are made. That is our reality.

The clue to this spiritual truth is the connective thread between the first and last books of the Bible. In Genesis 1:3 is God's first *expressed* act of creation, light: "Let there be light." But at the end of the Bible, Revelation tells us, "And the city has no need of sun or moon to shine on it, for the glory of God gives it light, and its lamp is the Lamb" (21:23 ESV). So the beginning of the Bible is the creation of light, and at the end of the biblical narrative God is saying that he, through Jesus Christ, is the light we must value above all other forms; that it is the only light we must look to as our fundamental source of illumination.

That confirms for me that God's first heralded act of creation, "Let there be light," was never just physical light. And certainly theologians have said as much, because according to Genesis, the sun and moon, our most visible lights, were created on day three. So perhaps all along the type of light God introduced was not the kind of light you can *see*, but the kind of light you can *know*. The kind of light of knowledge that led scientists like Lennox, McGrath, and others to a deeper faith, the light of law. And the kind of light of compassion that spoke to me in Cathy's house and broke through to my burdened heart, the light of love. This is the duality of light as law *and* love, rolled together as one. How could one source of light be both law and love? Because what I see in that phrase, "Let there be light," is God announcing *order*. Order, yes, that can be discerned, learned, and understood through scientific knowledge. But it is also the more ephemeral order that tells of the person of God, his grace, mercy, compassion, and wisdom. It is order flowing from God's very nature, giving us knowledge of him through our physical world and about who we are as beings made in his image. God was essentially introducing himself to us and binding himself to us.[10] In those words, "Let there be light," he is speaking to our minds and our hearts to *let* him in; for us to see the world's structure and harmony as his handiwork, that the heavens and the earth all testify to his being, and that we can look to their constancy as a source to strengthen our own faith that the God who created them will neither leave nor forsake us. Only a God of love *and* law could be so bold and so humble at the same time. He did not say, "Here is light, now bow down to it," or, "Here is light, take it or leave it." The presentation of light is like a gentle plea and a brazen directive all in the same phrase, never to be separated.

God's light, then, is who God is, his law *and* his love. Out of the mind of God, his character and his abundance, he created the world; his power, wisdom, and understanding (Jer. 51:15). And so his light is the order of the world that has been marching forward as that first burst of energy billions of years ago, or a few thousand years ago. It doesn't matter what you believe the time frame to be, because the main point is that God did it. And the initial model for that marching forward has been and always will be God's covenantal law: the Ten Commandments.

For many people today the Ten Commandments is an ancient relic whose display on public or government property is constantly being challenged. There's also the more entertaining reference in the famous movie, *The Ten Commandments*, starring Charlton Heston. But for the most part many of us see these laws as a sort of checklist of dos and don'ts we learned in Sunday school, but that are hard to apply to today's complicated daily life. However, it is imperative that we all readjust our thinking and see these commandments not as a relic but as an actual reality of how the world works, of how it is powered. The rest of the book will explain this idea in detail, but here is how to begin.

As I mentioned, for so long I only understood these ten laws as a moral code, almost like arbitrary bullet points in a PowerPoint presentation, showing how I measure up, judging whether or not I'm in good standing with God. But then I started thinking, *What if in addition to its moral moorings, we look also at its structure and design, as if it were a computer app?* Then we could overlay that design not only on us but also on the fixed laws of nature—the created world—to see if there are any similarities. If there is an alignment of the two, it could help paint a picture of the world "as it really is." It would also mean that the Ten Commandments are not arbitrary bullet points, but an actual template for *all* law. We could indeed see the world and everything in it as God's lighthouse, where his light—his law and his love—lives and thrives, providing both its engine and its fuel.

God's Lighthouse

But if it's right to compare God's Ten Commandments to a lighthouse, then there's something else that's necessary. In fact, the laws themselves are not in arbitrary order but rather have a hierarchy, not like a pyramid where the lower parts support the apex, but a lighthouse where one commandment defines the other nine's purpose for being, just as light defines a lighthouse. Thanks to Reverend Bucherri's insights, I do believe the Commandments' design has a strong physical resemblance to lighthouses.

The lighthouse lamp is a beacon on a high tower—Bucherri's "fire on a stick"—showing the way to safety as well as warning against danger. God's law given to Moses was announced out of a "consuming fire" atop a mountain, Mount Sinai (Ex. 24:17). Its purpose: to illuminate the way to freedom, to define a covenantal relationship with God, to help us navigate through any storm in life.

THE LIGHTHOUSE AND THE TEN COMMANDMENTS

These are the Ten Commandments.

1. "I am the LORD your God, who brought you out of Egypt, out of the land of slavery. You shall have no other gods before me." (Ex. 20: 2–3)
2. "You shall not make for yourself an image in the form of anything in heaven above or on the earth beneath or in the waters below." (v. 4)
3. "You shall not misuse the name of the LORD your God, for the LORD will not hold anyone guiltless who misuses his name." (v. 7)
4. "Remember the Sabbath day by keeping it holy." (v. 8)
5. "Honor your father and your mother, so that you may live long in the land the LORD your God is giving you." (v. 12)

Commandments 6 through 9 comprise the most known of the Decalogue, which I like to call the "thou shalt nots" as they appear in the King James Version.

1. "You shall not murder." (v. 13)
2. "You shall not commit adultery." (v. 14)
3. "You shall not steal." (v. 15)
4. "You shall not give false testimony against your neighbor." (v. 16)
5. "You shall not covet. . . ." (v. 17)

You'll see that the first four commandments describe our relationship to God, while the remaining commandments detail our relationship with God's creation. But take a closer look, because directing the course of *all* the laws is the first commandment. The first commandment is the "fire" on the stick, a blazing beacon presiding over the other laws, powering the engines of faith, igniting the flames of obedience. When any one of commandments two through ten is violated, it is because the first commandment had already been broken, a failure to keep God first; a failure to make the relationship with God so important and so vital that the other commandments are kept just by seeing the light of God's love, righteousness, and grace. Just as in the lighthouse—where the light gives the tower its defined purpose, its intentions clear—so it is with the first law; it defines the rest of the commandments, giving them a higher purpose, a reason to be kept. And as it applies to us, it provides motivation for not committing adultery, stealing, or lying, but rather seeing God in all his glory, to see his beauty, feel his love— that alone becomes more satisfying than any temporal temptation.

But as it applies to nature, it shows how *all* laws operate on this principle, that all things are ordered and defined by something, and that life itself is not arbitrary. This takes a much deeper look, one that comprises the journey of the rest of this book.

The power of the lighthouse is its subtle mimicking of the first commandment's authority over the other nine commands. The lighthouse's defining beacon mirrors God's omnipresence. It is where, for me, that tiny old photo of a lighthouse in Cathy's home is transformed from a "light on a stick" into a divine messenger. And its message goes right to the heart of how the world and everything in it began.

THREE PARTS—ONE GOD

The iconic words of Genesis boldly state, "In the beginning God created the heavens and the earth" (1:1). Those words mean that before there was anything, there was God: "In the beginning God . . ."[11] Perhaps it was

Aristotle's Immovable Mover or Thomas Aquinas's Uncaused Cause, which both point to some *thing* or some *one* that put the whole of creation on its path. But regardless, I accept as fact that there is a God, and that that God created the world, the heavens, and the earth in which we live.

Now the next question is, "*How* did God do it?"

It seems to me that a sovereign, triune God would really need just three elements to make a world; three because God is three in one: Father, Son, and Holy Spirit. Scripture tells us God created out of his own abundance, out of who God is. And if God is indeed triune as Christian doctrine says, and the world is in God's image, then the whole of the world, too, would mirror those three parts.

So here they are.

The first part is natural laws. These are hard-wired statutes, fundamental and fixed, that cannot be bargained with or altered; things like time, gravity, and electromagnetism. These rules can be studied and measured. They're like the framework for a building, providing stability. They give us consistency that we can rely on like the seasons and the length of days that are so important to our everyday lives.

The second part of God's created world is the sort of organic software, the ongoing creation, re-creation and growth. It would be a way for the world to flourish on its own, a form of growth that thrives within the framework, seemingly on its own but with a directive embedded deep within.

And the third part is a built-in way of sustaining the entire system, a way that constantly holds up what God has built; an act of worship, even more so a kind of mandated fealty, showing that everything in this world bows down to something, is defined by something.

All three of these ingredients interact seamlessly and mimic one overriding principle. And that's where the lighthouse imagery is most powerful: it stands for God's one law, "I am the Lord your God." Imagine this one light, shone through a divine prism lens, where its beam splits, refracting the Trinity into its three persons, where we see not just their titles but their *functions* in creating and sustaining our world.

The *Father* is the fixed law, collectively called the covenant. *Covenant* is a legal contract, but secured in blood. It is, by nature, a law born of love. For if there is a God of love who created the world, the stars, the heavens, and us, too, then we could look at the natural laws as covenants specifically, as laws created by a loving Father. We experience this covenant daily in architecture: the places we live, work, and play. Physical structures first and foremost must abide by the fixed laws of nature.

The *Son* functions as the second ingredient, the recreation and growth, which we will appropriately call the sacrifice. In our world, for something to be gained, something else must decrease, lessen, or even die. And the most basic example is agriculture: a garden. Seeds must die, in essence; they give up their original form to produce plants, just like the Son gave his life to transform humanity, to redeem us to God.

And finally, the *Holy Spirit* functions as the sustaining element of creation that I refer to as the glory. It is worship. It is the Spirit that holds something up as most important, something worthy of praise. Beautiful earthly examples are music and art. Those are two of the most powerful and mysterious means of expression in the world. Their power emanates from their physical nature, a nature that we humans did not create. Music takes our greatest longings and lets them soar to driving rhythms, beautiful melodies, and soothing harmonies. Whatever words or actions are put to music we not only remember better, but we will praise. Napoleon famously said, "Show me who controls the music in a society and I care not who makes its laws."

So here we have our world created by a loving God made with three driving forces: the covenant, the sacrifice, and the glory. All three encompass the totality of what the world is. The covenant, what is built; the sacrifice, what is grown; and the glory, what is worshipped. We will be coming back to these terms throughout the book. After all, they are the building blocks to everything in us and in the world.

Who we are in mind, body, and spirit mirrors who God is, in the Father, Son, and Holy Ghost; this is God's kingdom, his lighthouse.

But even still, knowing about God's world versus experiencing his power in our lives can be two separate things. So let me share with you a compelling lesson my brother Kenny taught me, about life and about death, about knowledge and about experience.

Kenny, the younger of my two older brothers, died in 2009 of cancer. A few years before his death, he was a virile and powerful man. He could bench press more than three hundred pounds and took great pride in his physical prowess. But he was also a great artist, a painter. Painting was like breathing to him. As long as I knew him, his artwork gave him a sense of identity, a reason to live. Even his wife and two daughters sometimes felt second to his art. But then came the cancer. It was a rare form that did not respond to chemotherapy. And the injections the doctors gave him prolonged his life but couldn't save it. Soon the cancer began to eat away his muscle flesh. He wasted away and began to look like a skeleton with skin. His eyes, sunken into his skull, looked too large for his head. At this point Kenny could no longer paint, he could not even walk; he could barely sit up; he could not do any of the things that had made his life worth living. He decided for himself that it was time to go into hospice care.

Unlike a cold hospital room with tubes and fluorescent lighting, hospice is a home, warm and welcoming, where family members can come and sit, or cry, or just be there. When the news came that Kenny was beginning to deteriorate quickly, I flew home to Minnesota from New York City to be with him. We didn't know how long he had and didn't want to think about it. After all, miracles can happen.

As I waited in the airport for my flight, I got a call from a friend at work. But our conversation that day was nothing about the news. He wanted to express his sympathy, knowing that my brother would die soon. We talked about this evil called cancer. I told him how I was certain that this disease is straight out of Satan's personal storehouse of hell. And I wondered how a loving God could allow such demonic forces to take my brother, or anyone's loved one, away.

Upon arriving in Minnesota, I went immediately to the hospice home. Little did I know that Kenny had also been on a journey of sorts. I'd expected to find him railing against the tides of bad luck, angry at the world and God. But instead he was calm and in the midst of an extraordinary relationship. Over the last few months he had met God. Oh, he had prayed to God before, had worshipped God. But until he had nothing left in life *but* God, that was when he really began to know God.

He said at the end of his life that the relationship had become so real to him, so all-consuming and sufficient, that despite all the other pleasures his life had been defined by, he would not trade more years of life for this opportunity of knowing God. That was how important it was. He had finally made it to the originating prism of the lighthouse. God's first commandment was as real to him as the air around him. And that was our comfort. The darkness of Satan had lost. God Almighty, his light of victory, would never be extinguished. I know that now.

Kenny will always be an inspiration to me. I will always carry his sentiment within my soul, that to know God is more powerful than any earthly pleasure. And this book is a dedication to his end-of-life revelation. But I don't want to wait until the end of my life to experience God. I want to do it now, in the everyday, to fully bask in God's ever-presence. And there is a way to do that through law and love, through natural order and the way things were meant to work, through covenant, sacrifice, and glory.

So this is our journey: to explore this lighthouse where God lives. To learn how to see, hear, and feel God in the everyday. To be assured—as I was in Cathy's summer home and as Kenny was as death approached—that a wilderness of life's troubles is nothing to fear, because it gives God an opportunity to show you his light, where we then can truly experience the joy and hope that is present when God alone is our living reality.

PART I

The Covenant

CHAPTER 2

Law Born of Love

Out of the mind of God the words, "Let there be light," and by them, a world is created.

I love life. I love its simplicity as well as its complexities and nuances. I love a summer rain, a fresh blanket of winter snow, a warm fall breeze, or a cool spring morning. I also enjoy lively conversations with friends or being alone with my thoughts. God has blessed me through this journey we call life, to have helped me grow into a centeredness and contentment, bringing me to a point where I now consider it a privilege to pray and an honor to be thankful; to know that no matter what earthly love I have or is taken from me, God's love still has value, is still precious.

But I have become more and more aware during my work covering religion that many people do not share my take on life. One question I'm continually asked is, "How could a loving God allow pain and suffering?" It is perhaps the most emotionally charged query of the human experience. If there's one thing that drives people away from believing in God, it is the seemingly unbridled presence of evil, of disease, of heartbreaking sorrow. If God is love like the gospel writer says, then how can these things be?

I'm thinking of recent headlines that provide plenty of examples. In the Middle East, Islamic terrorists target Christians and nonbelievers for extermination. A young woman, raped thirty times before noon, begs the Peshmerga soldiers battling ISIS to bomb her location, seeing death as her and her fellow refugees' only hope for freedom.

Here at home on U.S. soil, an all-too-frequent act of violence: a lone gunman with hate on his mind commits a mass killing.

But even discounting international affairs and violence in our communities, conflicts in our own homes are just as rampant. The home, which should be a haven of rest, becomes a battleground for strife, a house of dishonesty and despair. A husband has an affair because he's fallen out of love with his wife. A woman has an affair with a married man because she's convinced they are soul mates and his wife doesn't understand him. A single mother cries alone at night, unable to feed her child. The child's father left them for greener pastures, or had no intention of caring for the fruits of his lustful passions. Another child is sexually abused by the adult who should have protected her.

What is wrong here? Why is this world the way it is? I will try to pose an explanation that is at least plausible if not palatable. For, in this answer, lies the light of truth and compassion, law and love. It's the duality of light, displayed day after day right before our eyes.

A BROKEN WORLD

It may seem odd at first, but all of these tragedies happen for the same reason: this world is broken, and we are a broken people. A Christian often refers to this as a fallen world, and even atheists will acknowledge a world that is broken. And this brokenness has caused us to have what theologians call "disordered loves."[1] Disordered love makes a priority out of something that should not be a priority and puts its ultimate trust in that instead of the real source of love, God. We have come full circle back to the first commandment.

Here's a simple fable, a parable really, that might help illustrate this idea. It's the story of a loving father who makes a marvelous gift for his child. The father says to his son, "Son, this gift is unique and special. I am giving it to you because I love you so much."

The son says in response, "Oh, Father. I will cherish this gift always and take great care of it."

The father instructs the boy on how to take care of it properly. At first the boy, eager to please the father and in awe of the gift, obeys the father's every directive regarding the gift. But after a while, the gift no longer has the allure it once had. The boy begins to forget his father's careful mandates about how to care for it. Then one day, one of the boy's so-called friends who's jealous of the boy's present tells him, "I have something just like that. If you really want to get the most out it, I can show you ways that will be so much more fun. Why don't you try this way?"

And the boy says, "Oh, no! My father said I should never do that with it."

But the boy, intrigued by the other boy's so-called knowledge about the gift says, "Well, I guess once won't hurt." And so the boy ignores the father's important stipulation. But, as you know with all jealous friends' advice, it doesn't go well. And the boy says, "Oh, my beautiful gift! It's ruined!"

Now the gift no longer works the way it was intended. It is broken.

And so the wise father, already knowing the answer, asks the boy, "Did you do something to the gift I told you that you shouldn't?"

The son answers, "Yes, but it was my friend who showed me. He said he had one like it and it worked for him that way."

"My son," says the father, "I told you the gift was unique, it is one of a kind. And now it will take a very long time to fix. But I will repair and restore your gift that is broken."

You can almost feel the father's sadness. It's not only about the broken gift, but what caused the problem in the first place. His sorrow is because the boy put his trust in a lie, rather than in his father's truth. In so doing, he changed their relationship. In fixing the broken gift, the father will also work to restore the son's trust. And that is why it will take some time.

REPAIRING THE BROKENNESS

Our world was once perfect, but it is now broken. And if you want to blame someone, blame Adam and his wife Eve. They broke it. And they broke it in a way that it requires a long time and process to fix. And because we are all descendants of Adam, and part of the world's circuitry and vast materials, we are broken too. There is toxicity in our souls inherited from our ancient ancestor, Adam.

It's a metaphysical poison that the famous early-twentieth-century Christian commentator G. K. Chesterton wrote wittingly about in a rather unique essay. In responding to a question posed by *The Times* editor, "What's wrong with the world today?" Chesterton reportedly answered, "Dear Sir, I am."[2]

Chesterton, in his own sarcastic way, took responsibility for what's wrong in the world. That each of us on his or her own path of fear, self-centeredness, pride, and unforgiveness contributes in small and large ways to what's wrong in the world.

CREATING A WORLD

If it's difficult for you to trust in God because of the mess this world is in, I ask you to stop here for a moment and answer this question: What kind of world would a God of love create? Really think it through. If you read the theology of those who have done the intellectual heavy lifting, like Chesterton, C. S. Lewis, and Peter Hitchens for instance, you'll find that a God of love would create a world pretty much like the one we have. Please don't think that God wants murder and mayhem. God doesn't want our hearts to break. But the truth is scarier than fiction, and here's why. A God of love could only create a world of beings where loving him would be an option, a choice. Where doing his will, following his laws and designs for our lives could be rejected. True love cannot be coerced; it cannot be forced. True love means love as an act of your will, not as a byproduct of emotions, which can often lead us down a wrong path. This is how disordered loves get ahold of us and have control over us.

A Case Study

My sister had been married for about three years when she and her husband had a huge argument. At the time they lived down the block from where I lived with my parents while still attending college. She came storming into my parents' house one evening, saying she was done with her husband and wanted to go back and get her two toddlers. My wise mother, who was cooking at the stove, let my sister fume. I was busy sewing a dress at the kitchen table, and my sister plopped herself down, ranting about the grievous wrong she had endured. Always having a flair for the dramatic, her monologue was filled with impersonations, direct quotes (we had to take her word on that), and mimicry. My mother and I asked a few questions to clarify certain points, but never judged or sided with either party. After an hour or so, my mother said she was tired and went to bed. I stayed up sewing while my sister sat with me at the kitchen table. After a while, we started talking about other things: my summer attending a music camp and various other family events. Soon, she got tired too. And as if she had forgotten the vitriol of her earlier self, she got up and said, "Guess I'll go home now." No fanfare, no dramatic gestures, just a sleepy young woman wanting rest.

In the years since that evening, I've reflected on it often. I realize now that there were two parts to that story. The first is my sister's anger: raw emotion needing to vent, every fiber in her body feeling justified in their mode of action. The second part is something I've only lately understood, and that's her husband's love. He let her have the freedom to walk away— and the freedom to come back. Albeit, she slept on the couch that night but that event produced a deeper trust, a more permanent bond in their marriage. They have now been married for more than thirty-six years! In the end, any marriage is about the commitment itself, not about how we feel under certain circumstances. My sister and her husband had bound themselves in a legal commitment because of how they felt about each other, because they were in love. But in the end, what kept them in the commitment was the legal bond, which in effect made their love grow. Love created the path to the law of marriage, and the law strengthened their love.

Many of us can feel about God what my sister felt on that night about the man she was in a covenant bond to: very angry. But the pathway to returning to God is always there, the door is always open.

ANGER AND DISTRUST

A lot of us are angry with God. We're upset because our lives have not gone according to plan. Our plan. Hurt, pain, disappointments, tragedies have all contributed to our turning our backs on the God who created us. Blaming him, the Giver, because the gift is broken.

One of my theological mentors who has helped guide my spiritual walk is Dr. John Rankin, a professorial, mild-mannered man who runs the Theological Education Institute out of Connecticut. His greatest pleasure is taking on the hard questions people have about God and our culture, and he does it in such a way that is loving and quite brave, if you ask me. He once debated a lesbian activist about homosexuality in an auditorium packed with LGBTQ supporters! At the end of the night, many came up to him saying, "Even though I don't agree with you, I admire you for showing us respect and love." That's Dr. Rankin. He could just spew facts and show his intellectual superiority. But his goal is to win hearts as well as minds. So speaking the truth with love is the only option. He says, "You can win a debate, but lose the relationship."

I'm always amazed at his insights about people and knowledge about God. After every conversation with him I feel as if I've completed a seminary course. I'll never forget one thing he shared with me as we talked over coffee one afternoon. He said, "I have never met a true atheist. But I've met a lot of people who are angry at God." He went on to say that because we are all made in God's image, none of us escapes from the longing we have to be home with him, to be in that safe place of refuge. And those who profess a disbelief in God, even the most ardent, are at their core really just trying to control God, to make God in their image, to fix "the gift" their way. But unless we put our faith in the one Being who holds the proper tools to fix the brokenness, we are doomed to settle for temporary repairs.

PURE LOVE

It may be hard to imagine, considering the condition of the world, but this Being who possesses the tools to putting this world right has a lock on the one thing we're all looking for: pure love. Yes, love. And I say that mainly because I believe what the gospel writer John said, "God is love" (1 John 4:8). He didn't say, "God loves," as if it were only an action. He said God *is* love. God is the embodiment of love.

But this love is not the touchy-feely, passionate emotion we all fantasize about. I've discovered that there is an irony about the nature of love. All love, whether it's between parent and child, friends, or romantic partners is a paradox that we often miss, but that people like Dr. Rankin under-stand. And that is, true love creates boundaries. True love creates rules and parameters. Not prisons or iron locks and bars, mind you. True love binds, not to confine but to provide safety, which in turn lets us feel free. Just as the fence around a schoolyard keeps children safe from the outside world, from those who would prey on their innocence, so, too, that same fence sets the boundaries around where they can play safely and freely. No parent would look at that fence and say it is a prison. They would see it as a way for their children, their precious children, to play safely. It's the twist and winsomeness of love.

But this is where we can begin to understand why there's so much pain and sorrow. The playground fence is there because children don't always understand the dangers around them. They'll run after a ball into the street unless someone who's wiser drills into them the rules about never going outside the fence. It's for their protection.

What an adult is to a child, God is to adults. The knowledge and experience of a six-year-old is far less than that of his teacher. And in the same way, God is infinitely wiser and more knowledgeable than even the collective intelligence of everyone on earth. God's rules, his laws, are based on his love for us. Those who reject them run the risk of the dangers that any child would face running into a street after a stray ball.

Now, multiply that exponentially since the beginning of time and you may begin to see why our world is in the shape it's in. We have put our desire for "the ball," or things, or people above our love or desire for God or his rules, and we have blamed him for the mess that we've created.

God's love is a reality of divine light in the world. How can we be certain? Here's how.

The God of love that Scriptures describe speaks a language of love that is often expressed through law. The language is far more complicated than we'd ever expect, and yet, it's incredibly coherent. From Genesis to Revelation, God speaks in one basic love language called a covenant. This language speaks to us continually from God's two most prominent means of communication: the holy Scriptures and his nature all around us.

CREATION COVENANT

Since the beginning of time God has been speaking in covenants. As one writer said, the whole narrative of the Bible is a chronicle of covenants, one after another. God has bound himself to us and to creation through a covenantal relationship.[3] A covenant is a kind of legal contract, but instead of just being a written document, it bursts forth as a spiritual and physical reality too. Ancient covenants were forged in blood; that's how serious they were. (God, too, has forged a covenant with us through blood, but more on that in the next section.)

For right now, know that a covenant is not just about rules and regulations but fervent obedience, heartfelt desires we can actually experience, just like the covenant of marriage. Covenants could be between two equal partners, as in a marriage. Or, a covenant could be between unequal parties, like a king and a servant. And in the case of God's covenants, they are laws underwritten by love, because God is love, "the unfathomable source of all causality."[4]

Covenant Overview

The highlight reel of covenants in the Bible would feature Adam, Noah, Abraham, Moses, and King David. Each successive covenant adds more understanding to who God is and who we are in relation to him; every covenant is a new juncture and chapter in that relationship, and a new signpost to how God is working to "fix" the gift that was broken. Although the covenants appear to be different—Adam and the garden, Noah and the flood, Abraham and his son's sacrifice—they all express a basic formula of God saying, "I will be your God: You will be my people."[5]

But the first covenant in the Bible often gets overlooked as a covenant, because the word *covenant* never appears. But it has all the earmarks of a covenant. It is an extremely important covenant because it affects us all and cannot be bargained with or avoided, as we all live under its statutes and parameters. It's God casting his net as wide as possible so that all of us would be subject to his love and his protection, whether or not we want it, whether or not we acknowledge it.

Covenant of Creation

It's the covenant of creation itself: nature's laws. And it's stated in the first words of Genesis, "In the beginning God created the heavens and the earth" (1:1).

There are at least three ways we can know that God intends for us to understand creation itself as a covenant. The first is that God never has casual relationships with things or people. They are always serious, always binding.

You and I may have acquaintances or draw boundaries between Facebook friends, LinkedIn folks, family, BFFs, and people we just hang out with. But for God, relationships are not casual.

The second way we can know creation is a covenant is that Scripture itself is filled with either indirect or direct references of creation being a covenant, as in the book of Psalms, "The heavens declare the glory of God; the skies proclaim the work of his hands. Day after day they pour forth speech; night after night they reveal knowledge" (19:1–2). Or, as in Jeremiah 33:20, "If you can break my covenant with the day and my covenant with the night," saying that the motions of the sun and the earth, which create our day and night, are, in fact, part of his covenant.

CREATION'S COVENANTAL CONTRACT

The third way we can know creation is a covenant. And I think it has incredible wow factor. It's because the opening words of Genesis, the words every child in Sunday school learns, read like a preamble to a legal contract! It follows the pattern of most ancient contracts drawn up between a great king and a lesser vassal, where the introduction establishes a king's authority, power, and omnipotence.[6] This preamble at the opening of Genesis basically says, "This is God. There is nothing before God. He is the beginning. He created the world and everything in it. That's all we need say." It's simple and direct, no overstating of the facts. Then the next words are the historical context, describing the situation, a world of nothing without form, void. It's the "lesser vassal," and God's movements over that nothing. Then come God's first words, his first act as Creator and King. "God said, 'Let there be light' and there was light" (Gen. 1:3). It's the ignition. It's the spark. It's the fire on the stick, the divine match that set off the explosion, the Big Bang that put everything in motion. It's God as the flame and the fuel that from here on will always be a part of creation. Everything that came into being and continues to come into being carries a trace memory of this act. Even us. A recent news story explained that for the first time ever scientists have witnessed the moment of conception, a "bright flash of light." They captured on film "an explosion of tiny sparks" erupting from the egg at the exact moment that human life begins.[7] It is the constant recapitulation of God's creative act, "Let there be light." And proof that we are made to reflect his image. Which makes this covenantal contract unfolding in Genesis all the more important for us.

SCIENTIFIC INQUIRY

For the following explanation, I would like to lay aside the controversy over whether God created the world in six literal days or a gradual evolutionary process, as it will serve no purpose here. Instead, let's think of those seven days, the days of the creation account in Genesis, as the laying out of a covenantal document. Remember the basic formula is God saying, "I will be your God, and you will be my people." So those seven days are seven bullet points on a legal contract created by a loving God. The first day separating light from darkness; the second day separating the waters; the third day, land, vegetation, and seed bearing plants; the fourth day, the sun, the moon, and the stars; the fifth day, living creatures, fish of the sea, land animals, and birds; the sixth day, humanity, the making of "mankind in our image" (Gen. 1:26). And the seventh day, God rested. "And God saw that it was good" (v. 25).

REASONS TO BELIEVE

I like to think of the first chapter of Genesis as a poetic description of the contract for natural laws. And for this, I have Dr. Hugh Ross to thank. He is the president and founder of Reasons to Believe.

Dr. Ross is one of those quiet, brainy people who seems like a regular Joe, until he starts spouting physics equations for complex planet movements. He was an agnostic who later found his Christian faith by analyzing the biblical narrative through the lens of a scientist's sensibilities.

As we sat in my office, he told me, "I first tried to find him [God] in the philosophers of the world, Immanuel Kant, Descartes and others . . . and realized they had wrong concepts of space and time and universe. And that's what led me to actually begin to look at the world's holy books."

Dr. Ross heard all the arguments about the Bible being allegory at best or a complete fantasy at worst. But then he saw something in the account of creation that rocked his world. He said it was something that no other religion's holy book got right.

Dr. Ross told me: The Hindu's Vedas failed to do it. The Buddhist commentaries failed, the Koran failed, the Book of Mormon failed, B'hai faith failed . . . and finally, he picked up a Bible.

This ancient writing, the book of Genesis, the first book in the Bible, written several thousand years ago, accurately described the exact sequence of the evolutionary process. Whether it took place over days or billions of years, the flow of how the world came to be is mapped out exactly as scientists understand it. The sequence is first the water, then the first organisms appear; then the fish, the flora and fauna, the animals; and the last part of creation: us, the soul-bearing beings. It all fits, just as science has discovered.

Dr. Ross said he realized he was dealing with a document whose author either had incredible foreknowledge of scientific discovery or had a revelation from the Sovereign who created the world.

"Right away I realized this book was different than what I read in the philosophers'. It was different from what I read in the other holy books. Everything was clear. It was direct; specific statements about science, history, and geography, things that could easily be put to rigorous testing. And I think what alone caught my attention: the Bible alone commanded testing."

Those are the words of First Thessalonians that piqued his scientist's mind. It's a command as well as a challenge to "test all things" (1 Thess. 5:21 NKJV). It's an urging in Scripture to test its truthfulness and veracity. God doesn't want blind faith, but faith grounded in knowledge (Prov. 19:2). And knowledge about God can be found in the world he created.

God Builds His World

God may be done with the work of creating, but he is still active in the world he created. God, the great architect and builder, in that initial burst of light created all that was needed to construct his world. This entire universe of natural laws is his tool chest. In that one act, he created all he would need to fix it if it ever broke. He was prepared for all possibilities.

Within God's creation are not only the tools with which he is fixing this world, but they're also the tools we can look to, that God has given us to help him in the process. But, we have to have the instructions. For that, it's a good idea to take a look at the covenant God made with one of the superstars of the Old Testament, Moses.

The Covenant of Ten Commandments

The grandest moment of covenantal action in the Old Testament comes on Mount Sinai, when God, through the flaming bush, gives to Moses the Ten Commandments. This is a legal document by all means. These are laws laid out one by one. But it is also a more spiritual form of the creation of the world. It's a parallel version of the words, "Let there be light," God's call to order. But instead of "Let there be light," God's first commandment is, "I am the LORD your God, who brought you out of Egypt, out of the land of slavery. You shall have no other gods before me" (Ex. 20:2–3).

So in that first commandment, God was saying more emphatically, more forcefully that he is God, Creator of the heavens and the earth. He said the same thing at the beginning of creation, "Let there be light." But now there is no gentle plea, only the brazen directive to the people who have been chosen, through his promise to Abraham, to be a people holy unto himself. So he speaks more explicitly. He does not mince words. The net is not cast so wide now, but narrow, to a specific group of people, Jacob's family, the tribes of Israel.

Now in my Sunday school days at St. Peter's AME Church in Minneapolis,

I was taught about the Ten Commandments. To the Sunday school teacher's credit, she did the best she could with a class of rambunctious kids who were glad they didn't have to sit through a long sermon with the adults in the sanctuary. (Besides, we got treats!)

As we learned the Decalogue, we memorized as many as we could with no thought to order or importance. But we also assumed, because no one said otherwise, that when God gave his law to the Israelites, he was creating them on the spot, or very recently, as if to say, "Well, I've been mulling over what I wanted to tell you folks, and now that you're free and I have your full attention, here's what I came up with. Check it out and see what you think."

No. These commandments do have an order of importance, and they all bow to the first commandment, to keeping God first, keeping God as the light, the fire on the stick.

How can we know this for certain? There are a couple of ways. First, Christians can point to Jesus and how, when he was challenged to say which of the commandments is most important, he said, "Love the Lord your God with all your heart and with all your soul and with all your strength and with all your mind" (Luke 10:27). The second commandment is to love others as you love yourself. This is sometimes called the Golden Rule. Jesus said these two encapsulate all the commandments. The first four are about a relationship with God. The remaining represent relationship with God's creation. But all are dependent on keeping God first.

Before the Bush Burns

The second way to know the utmost importance of this first command is because of something else that happened when God spoke to Moses through the burning bush, before the Israelites got their freedom from slavery: God revealed for the first time in the Bible who he is.

Not until this point in the biblical narrative does God expose himself, name himself. It happened in Exodus 3:13–14, when God told Moses that he was sending him to Egypt to demand that Pharaoh let the Hebrews go.

Moses asked God, "Who shall I tell them is sending me?" In other words, "What is your name?"

The Hebrew answer is hard to translate, but it is the verb "to be." In most Bibles it's stated, "I Am." "Tell the Israelites, 'I AM' has sent you." This is not a lesson in conjugating verbs. This is God stating that he is existence itself. He is all powerful, omnipotent; he is all knowing, omniscient; and he is ever present, omnipresent. He is the reason there is even a *here* here or a *there* there; or even a *was* and a *will be*. He is the Alpha and Omega, the Beginning and the End, and everything in between.

The Ten Commandments are more than arbitrary laws compiled by a great prophet and patriarch. They are a description of who God is, arranged in a specific way, with this blaze of existential power lighting the way that gives us insight as to how the world functions. It's a template showing that everything in the world is dependent on something else. Nothing stands alone. God has left the mark of this incredible covenant on us all, and on all of creation, because, as we will learn in the next chapter, we all live in God's house. Let us now see how that house becomes a home.

CHAPTER 3

A House, a Home

The beauty of the house is order,
The blessing of the house is contentment,
The glory of the house is hospitality,
The crown of the house is godliness.

—AUTHOR UNKNOWN

I LOVE THESE WORDS. I FIRST SAW THEM FRAMED IN
needlepoint at my friend Cathy's summerhouse on the eastern end of Long
Island. And it certainly describes her house, especially its orderliness. The
dinner plates, saucers, and cups in the kitchen cupboards are arranged and
stacked with almost military precision; the beds in each room all have clean
sheets and pillowcases folded at the foot with pillows at the heads, ready
for the next occupant to make his or her bed. From that orderliness flows
a contentment that gives one the feeling that everything is rightfully in its
place, including anyone entering its portals. From family and friends to the
friars and sisters who make retreats in the house, there's a welcoming spirit
of the divine.

Mulling over the needlepoint's words, I sensed they describe much more than a house. They depict the necessary building blocks for creating a home: order, contentment, hospitality, and godliness. They form the frame for what we all crave, a loving place in which to dwell, a place where we can be. As one pastor said, "Home is to be naked and unafraid."[1] It's an abode where we unabashedly expose our true selves, and yet know we are overwhelmingly accepted and loved. And because of that there's no need to adorn ourselves with fig leaves like social status, accomplishments, or good looks to conceal our fears and frailties because we have none, at least none that control us. And as I thought even harder about these words, I realized they detail so much more than a place to come to, but a way of being.

For in these four attributes—order, contentment, hospitality, and godliness—lay not only the description of the homes and communities we strive to create and live in, but also the template from which they were originally fashioned: God's house, the heavens and the earth. Whether or not we acknowledge it or are aware of it, God's house begins with the rational order of creation, the covenant of love and its laws. It is here where we will find the light, the knowledge of what turns a house into a home.

A HOME

You see, *home* is sacred; whether it is our common home, the earth, as Pope Francis called it in his encyclical on the environment, or the homes we grew up in. I do believe that the idea of home holds a seminal place within our psyche. Perhaps it's part of a "pervasive longing we share" to "get back to the garden," God's Eden.[2]

Here's an encounter that convinced me of this at least. An elderly woman I'm quite close to began talking about the other home she had, even though she's lived in the same house for more than sixty-five years. She kept insisting she had another one that looked just like the one she was in. Everyone around her, from her adult son to close relatives and friends, kept telling her she *was* home. She kept insisting, "No, there's another house." I heard her say once to her son, "I'll pack my things so we can go home now."

Or, "What home are we going to?" I was so concerned that this was a sure sign of dementia and Alzheimer's disease. When she had an evaluation of her cognitive abilities, the doctor said that at eighty-eight years old, she was right in the normal range for someone her age.

"Normal!" I said.

"Yes," said the doctor.

"What about this talk of another house?" I asked.

The doctor said, "It's quite common for elderly people to talk of another home. Some doctors believe it may be that the person is longing for their childhood home. But no one's quite sure."

So I asked the doctor, "Could there be a spiritual reason?"

"What do you mean?" she asked.

"Well," I said, "could this be a universal desire to be at home with God, a longing that begins to show itself as life winds down?"

The doctor answered, "It's an interesting thought. Could be. But there would be no way to empirically test the theory."

The story may not be as convincing to you, but, regardless, we all seem able at least to relate to Dorothy's quest to get back home from the Land of Oz. The magical, mesmerizing beauty and wonders of Oz could not compete with the common cornfields of Kansas. Dorothy helped us learn that "there's no place like home" and that we need not venture beyond its physical boundaries to find our hearts' true desires.

A House Is Not Necessarily a Home

Many homes are houses, but not all houses are homes. I have an apartment in New York City where I live, but I always think of Minnesota as my home, even though I've lived in the Big Apple for more than twenty years. While all of us live in God's house, the heavens and the earth, not all of us live at home with God, which means being in a close relationship with him. God's house is perfectly ordered through the natural laws. But living at home with God requires a wholly different way of being. It's the godliness the needlepoint speaks of. It is making God your fortress and refuge. It means dwelling in the shelter of "the Most High" and finding "rest in the shadow of the Almighty" (Ps. 91:1).

GOD BUILDS HIS HOUSE

Don't take for granted why we call churches and temples houses of God. There's something much more profound at work here, because it's a microcosm of a larger context we are to grasp. The ancient Jewish temple had a specific design. It wasn't just an earthly architect's talents on display. Scholars believe that the Jewish temple built by King Solomon was made in the image of the cosmos. The columns, the water basins, the Holy of Holies, "every one of these objects is intended to recall and represent the universe."[3] It acknowledged that although we worship in buildings, God's house is really the whole of creation. And the order of God's house begins with God: "In the beginning God . . ."

Think about it for a moment. Look around you. All that you see, hear, and know can chart their beginnings back to this moment. Every building, structure, mountain, and mole hill; every computer, technological gadgetry; every person, animal, and insect; every sound, strains of music, blade of grass can trace the pathway of its origins back to that one moment in time when God said, "Let there be light." Even time itself is created here. Everything came about because of that one instant, that one divine decree.

IN SEARCH OF "THE GOD PARTICLE"

My search to better understand that phrase, "In the beginning," led me to Dr. William Lane Craig, a professor of Philosophy at Talbot School of Theology at Houston Baptist University in Texas. He's an analytic philosopher, which means he's trained in math and science. He explores not just *how* things happen, which is science, but the *why* behind them, which is philosophy and religion. We've only met once in person, when I interviewed him in the Fox studios. But we've had many conversations over the phone. His primary focus is defending a theological argument for the existence of a Creator God. The argument has three brief points:

1. Whatever begins to exist has a cause.
2. The universe began to exist.
3. Therefore, the universe has a cause.

The conclusion then is, "And since the universe can't cause itself, its cause must be beyond the space-time universe. It must be spaceless, timeless, immaterial, uncaused, and unimaginably powerful. Much like . . . God."[4]

I contacted Dr. Craig when the big news came from the CERN (European Organization for Nuclear Research) collider in Switzerland about the scientific discovery of the so-called God particle, also known as the Higgs boson particle, named after physicist Peter Higgs, one of six scientists who postulated its existence.

Although Dr. Craig is a philosopher by name, he is well versed in particle physics, and so was able to explain in laymen's terms what the Higgs boson discovery actually was and why it was nicknamed the God particle.

FUNDAMENTAL FORCES

At first my eyes glazed over as he launched into his explanation of particle physics, which is a branch of physics that studies "the fundamental constituents of matter," the subatomic constituents or the small stuff like quarks, leptons, and photons.[5] It was a reminder to me of those school years when I developed that deer-in-the-headlights look during some of the more intense lectures. I always found the subject matter fascinating but challenging.

But Dr. Craig was able to take it down a few notches and help me understand the information to the point where it let me see more clearly how it relates to a Creator God. And he helped me see that there's a payoff to understanding this point of particle physics.

As far as the God particle goes, Dr. Craig explained, "there's what's known as the Standard Model for particle physics." The Standard Model, he said, "is a model of the particles and the forces that govern them." There are four fundamental forces of nature: the strong force, the weak force, the electromagnetic force, and gravity. The Standard Model is concerned with only three of those forces: the strong force, the weak force, and the electromagnetic force.

Gravity is not included.

To understand that, we must go back to what's happening "In the beginning . . ."

THE BEGINNING EXPLAINED

Dr. Craig explained to me that "when the universe begins, it begins in this symmetrical state in which the four forces of nature are all combined together." But then, he said, "what happens is, as the universe expands and cools, these symmetries are broken and these forces begin to separate out. And the first that comes out is gravity."

This happens within the first milliseconds after the Big Bang.

Even though gravity is fundamental to our world, it doesn't belong with the other three forces because it left the building, so to speak, early in the process. So that Standard Model of particle physics only deals with the three forces that stuck together longer.

So within this Standard Model there are, said Dr. Craig, "all sorts of various particles that are postulated to exist like the photon and the electron and the neutrinos. . . . And all of these particles have been verified experimentally." They have been detected using these big colliders. "But the last particle in the Standard Model to be detected empirically is this Higgs boson. The particle is very massive and so it requires enormous energy to create. It's too difficult to reproduce in a collider. . . . It decays almost immediately," he said.[6]

Why Call It God?

So why is the Higgs boson particle called the God particle?

Dr. Craig says it was a name coined by physicist Leon Lederman who wrote a book in 1993 called *The God Particle*. He named it so for two reasons. "First of all, just as God underlies the existence of the physical universe and sustains it in being, so does the Higgs particle underlay the existence of the physical objects in the universe, because it is the particle that imparts to [the other particles] their various masses" by creating "a field permeating space. . . . As other particles move through this field, they acquire their various masses. And so Lederman made the analogy between that and the way God underlies all of physical reality by conserving it, and upholding it by being, moment by moment.

"And the second reason Lederman called it the God particle is, I think, very amusing," said Dr. Craig, "and that is because it is so difficult to detect. You can't see God with the five senses. You can't hear him, see him, smell him, or touch him, and yet he's there. And similarly the Higgs particle can't be detected easily. It's frustratingly, exasperatingly difficult to detect. It took decades to find it. And yet, it's still there. It's pervasive in its influence. It affects every physical object that exists, even though you may not be able to see and touch it.

"And yet the lesson of the God Particle is that just because you don't see [it], you don't detect it, doesn't mean that it isn't there and isn't pervasive even in its influence. Even though you may not see God's providential plan for your life or for history, God is still objectively there and at work guiding the universe towards his pre-vision ends.

"I rather like the label," said Dr. Craig, "because it reminds us [of] these two important theological truths: God's conservation of the world in being and God's objective existence even when he's hidden."[7]

It sounds to me almost like a game of Bunkum! Except for one thing. In Bunkum, the hidden object is perfectly visible to the naked eye. The Higgs boson particle is not. But it does show how we all live in the broader sense of God's house.

SCIENCE HAS NO "THEORY OF EVERYTHING"

One point that Dr. Craig made about the Higgs boson particle is quite important: it neither proves nor disproves God's existence. One reason is its appearance on the scene following the Big Bang happened after things began to cool down, after gravity had left the party. If gravity isn't included, as it is not in the Standard Model for physics, then it can't be a "theory of everything," a sort of God-like scientific explanation of how the entire world works. It can't answer the bigger philosophical questions such as, "Why are we here?" "Why do we even exist?" And there's another curious question that scientists like Dr. Craig ponder: "Why do our mathematical models work?" In other words, "Why," as Dr. Craig said, "should the universe have the language of mathematics written throughout its structure? Why would it be this rational, orderly universe that's amenable to experimental discovery?"

Here may be a better clue to God's covenantal laws that we can actually see at work: math!

ARCHITECTURE: A MATHEMATICAL PATH TO LIVING IN GOD'S HOME

There's no other perfect visual model of mathematical certainty than architecture. Mathematical laws dictate fundamental facts about how a structure should be constructed. The most fundamental law governing how buildings are built is the law of gravity, that first of the four forces to separate itself out after the Big Bang. It's the most pervasive and fundamental law governing the universe. Here, we see God's providential wisdom at work. That gravity would be the first of the four forces to separate itself out of the dense hotness of the beginning of time points to a covenantal force that cannot be bargained with. Regardless of the architect's intentions, God's requirement through gravity means that even if a builder does not believe in God, God has put something in the natural law that the architect must put his faith in so that the structure will not fall down.

Pythagoras and His Theorem

It was in a conversation with Dr. Michio Kaku that I began to see this authority in architecture as I'd never seen it before. Here was God truly hiding in plain sight. Dr. Kaku is not a particularly religious person. He's a theoretical physicist who's kind of a rock star in the science world. He has an incredible mind and looks at things a little bit differently. Even from a young age, he asked questions most adults couldn't come up with. He tells the story of when he was six years old and looking at a pond with fish in it, wondering if the fish understood there was a whole world outside their pond.

I've interviewed Dr. Kaku a couple of times about new scientific finds in the universe. And I've asked him about my thesis: that for all systems or things, whether they're animal, vegetable, or mineral, there is a seminal point, a light that defines them. I didn't tell him that I thought this seminal point was trace material of the divine and sovereign God's law, the first commandment. I wanted to see what he thought about just the idea of this existing.

He told me that as far as architecture is concerned, his theory is that all buildings are held up by the Pythagorean theorem. Whether it's a cathedral or a country shack, a house or a hut, a tower or a temple, all buildings are held up by the mathematical relationship expressed in the theorem first discovered by Pythagoras in the sixth century BC. We'll revisit Pythagoras in later chapters; he has a lot to do with how we understand music too. But for right now let's focus on pure mathematics and why Dr. Kaku could give his theorem such credit for understanding how buildings stay put.

The Pythagorean theorem is a mathematical equation for right triangles, meaning a triangle (a three-sided shape) with one 90-degree angle, the L shaped angle. Most high school students learn the equation in geometry class, while many older folks like myself remember the name but not the reason behind it.

The theorem's equation states that A squared plus B squared equals C squared. Square means any number times itself, like two times two (which equals four) or five times five (which equals twenty-five) for example. And the A, B, and C represent each side of the triangle. A and B are the vertical and horizontal lines that form the right angle (90 degrees). And C is the line that stretches between them called the hypotenuse. Like most mathematical equations, they are not invented, they were simply discovered, which is, as Dr. Craig pointed out, one of the fascinations of this world: why math works. No matter the length of A and B, the total of their squared sides will equal the square of the line C. Why should it work? It is just one of those fun facts about this physical world that I, and others, believe points to a Creator God, one who is a mathematician!

If Michio Kaku's assessment of the Pythagorean theorem is correct, then the right angle, four of which forms a cross of perpendicular lines, is literally holding up every building and structure. The implication is that whether or not you're a Christian or believe in any religion, the cross—the Christian symbol upon which Jesus was crucified—is the supporting structure of everything that we build.

I decided to test this theory with someone else who not only knows architecture but teaches it.

THE ANGLE AND THE CROSS

Randall Ott is the dean of the School of Architecture and Planning at Catholic University in Washington, D.C. I first met him when I covered the papal visit of Pope Benedict XVI. Catholic University was one of the spots on the pope's agenda, and I was looking for interesting sidebar stories to fill out our coverage. Catholic University's architecture school is one of the best in the country, and many non-Catholic students study there simply because it rates as a great school, not just a great Catholic school. The technological rules for designing and building a structure are the same whether you're Catholic, Muslim, Hindu, or atheist. Gravity is gravity is gravity. Matter is matter. How the two interact here on earth is based on facts that no religion may alter. And so I sought out Randall Ott to ask about Michio Kaku's statement that all buildings are based on the Pythagorean theorem.

At first Randall said he didn't believe it. In fact, he said, "It's incorrect."

But Randall assumed Michio was talking about proportionality, "one of the fundamentals of architecture," he said. Proportionality is especially true in a Western context, he said, "emanating down from Greece through Vitruvius . . . the most well-known of the Roman writers on architecture. It picked up big-time in the Renaissance and became later for Renaissance Italian architecture very much an overarching concern. And that certainly did impact a lot of Western architecture because proportional systems are critical in terms of composition. It's one thing we teach."[8]

So it seemed Randall didn't agree with the theoretical physicist about the Pythagorean theorem because he only equated it with design features, not structural necessity. But then I explained it a bit differently. I told him the idea that the Pythagorean theorem existed in all architectural structures was based on the idea that the right-angle triangle, whether explicitly or implicitly, had to be present. I used the example of harmony in music because there are similarities; both are mathematically based. Because of the mathematical relationship between different notes (explained more in chapter 9), you don't have to play all the notes of a chord in order to recognize what chord it is as long as you have certain other information about its harmonic base. For example, you can play two notes of a triad chord, and you can still identify the chord, because the third note of the triad is harmonically implied. It's the same idea behind Michio Kaku's statement about the Pythagorean theorem in architecture. Because of the relationship between the structure's angles, it's implied; it's there holding the structure in place even though there's no visible right angle—in other words, a cross shape. But it's still there holding things up.

Randall then said, "I think that makes sense. I see it. I would agree with him there, in the kind of inherent stability [that] is essential in a building and will always be when it's going to get built, or [else] it's going to come down on somebody."

So, what this means for me is that a mathematical fact governing architecture is tied to the fundamental symbol of Christianity: the cross.

BIBLICAL BUILDING

With this information, I now take greater interest in the Bible's building projects. There are a few that stand out, such as the Tower of Babel, Noah's ark, and the building of the temple. But to tie in to what Michio Kaku and Randall Ott helped confirm about the Pythagorean theorem and the cross, I turn now to what is probably the most famous architectural reference in Christianity: "The stone the builders rejected has become the cornerstone" (Luke 20:17; Acts 4:11; 1 Peter 2:7).

It's mentioned first in the Old Testament. Christians believe the Old Testament writers were predicting the coming of the Messiah, Jesus, where in the New Testament it is fulfilled in Mark 12:10, "Haven't you read this passage of Scripture: 'The stone the builders rejected has become the cornerstone'?"

The cornerstone of a building is what is laid perfectly straight and level and becomes the defining reference point for the rest of the stones when they are laid. Today builders and "Do It Yourselfers" can go to any home improvement store and get a level to make sure that first brick or piece of tile is even. If it is not, the whole project will be off kilter. If you're laying a patio or tiling a bathroom, it will just look bad, as well as unprofessional. But if you're building a house, bridge, or skyscraper, the result could be more serious. The building could eventually fall or have to be dismantled.

Today, even though we understand the concept of the cornerstone, architects use computers to work through the mathematical equations that will ensure a building doesn't fall down. It also helps them create structures that are far from looking like squares and rectangles. In Manhattan there's a tall building that looks as though it were twisting in a dance. The Sydney Opera House looks like a giant sea creature. And London has some of the most unusually shaped modern buildings I have ever seen. Though no visual cornerstones were used, per se, their ability to remain standing relies on unseen weights and counterweights, like underground supports.

When the biblical writers talked about cornerstones, they were using references that people understood. A mathematical equation such as A squared plus B squared equals C squared was not part of their lexicon of information, even if they lived after 600 BC when Pythagoras discovered it. Most people had a basic understanding of how things were built. But if Michio Kaku's theory is correct, and Randall Ott says it is, then the cornerstone helped establish the implied presence of the theorem, and hence the implied presence of the cross. For what is a cross but four right triangles; each quadrant of the triangle speaking the law of the first commandment in the form of the Pythagoras theorem? In the form of a fixed point of light, the Pythagorean theorem exclaims loud and clear in scientific vernacular the wisdom of Solomon, "Unless the LORD builds the house, the builders labor in vain" (Ps. 127:1). It shouts the directive of the first commandment, "I am the LORD your God . . . you shall have no other gods before me" (Ex. 20:2–3). It is the lamp of the lighthouse once again speaking to us through the rules of what is built. God, the Master Architect, will never give his glory to another (Isa. 42:8). Obey the law, or the building crumbles; the structure will not stand.

Every time I look at buildings and structures today, I see crosses everywhere; in the window frames, the scaffolding, the crown molding, a telephone pole. Either the cross is implied, as it is in a door or a window frame, or it is explicit, as in the trusses of a suspension bridge.

Every synagogue and temple, every mosque, office tower, cabin, house, shack, shelf, dinner table, side table, bed, chair is being held up by the cross. You can cover up a cross in a church to hold your high school graduation ceremony, or to make your presidential speech; you can deny God in classrooms or politics, but the cross is still present, holding up every structure, every platform. God must be chuckling at us, like a parent watching a toddler who is convinced he can drive a car even though his feet can't reach the pedals.

Even trees growing up from the soil must abide by the principle of Pythagoras's equation. Their roots must be deep enough to offset the angle by which a tree's trunk and branches stretch upward and outward. Gravity has dictated that even the world of nature abides by certain mathematical principles; principles that we can discover and work with, but never change or alter to suit our needs.

God, the Master Architect, formed the laws that all buildings must follow. Through a simple, "hidden in plain sight" mathematical fact, objective and rational, he has shown us how to build with structural integrity: a cross. And at the same time, he has given us the tools to make a home of spiritual strength: also, the cross. Its dual purpose, like the duality of light, is a sign of a deep bond with the great Creator. He chose that the cross, in his cosmic game of Bunkum, would be hiding in plain sight for all to see.

And just as God made choices as to how to build his world, we, too, make choices to build our own lives.

PRINCIPLES OF BUILDING

You see there's a lot we can learn about building our own lives from the principles of architecture. First, from a purely physical perspective, the human body has a skeleton and bone structure. A building, too, has a framework of wood or steel; the roofline with its beams jutting evenly from a long chord resembles our own spinal column and rib cage. Our organs—heart, lungs, kidneys, and others—that keep us alive by regulating the flow of blood and oxygen could coincide with the central electrical and plumbing systems that help a house sustain life through heating, air-conditioning, and waste management. Buildings have siding, a protective layer of skin just like our bodies.

We are both built according to a plan, a design. All buildings, from the simple to the complex, are built according to a builder's, or an architect's, specifications. The square footage, the materials used, the location, the style are all decided by someone. The building doesn't design itself nor build itself.

For us, well, even those who are skeptical of the idea of God being the designer of humanity and life must acknowledge that much of who we are was decided by someone else. You did not choose how tall you are, your hair color (natural hair color, that is), or your skin color; where you were born, or who gave you birth. Those parts were decided for you.

But unlike a building, we have the ability to alter the course of our lives.

We can follow the Architect's plans, renovating and updating according to his specifications. And if we do, we move toward greater stability. Or we can go it alone, pay no heed to the Architect's original plan, and risk moving toward increased instability. And this is where our spiritual lessons from architecture begin, as the Master Architect has given us through what is built.

All buildings are made for a purpose. Whether they're houses of worship, office towers, sports arenas, or homes, there's a reason, a functional purpose to their existence. Buildings can be beautiful, and many are, but they are not constructed solely to be an object of beauty. They can even have facades that mask their purpose. But no building can fulfill its purpose unless it rests on a firm foundation with a cornerstone that's either implied or explicitly present.

Now, let's see through the prism of purpose how covenants build our lives of increased stability, or instability. Of greater freedom, or greater enslavement.

CHAPTER 4

A Temple and the Choices We Make

To his own master he stands or falls.

—ROMANS 14:4 NKJV

BUILT FOR A PURPOSE

I count Pastor Rick Warren as a friend. He runs Saddleback Church in Southern California, a megachurch with about twenty thousand members. To folks outside of the church world he's most known for writing the best-selling (mega-selling) book, *The Purpose Driven Life*, which chronicles how we were made for God's pleasure. Whatever we pursue, be it music, journalism, law, or finance, we must understand that all these vocations provide a means to serving God. The choices we make when we build our careers or our families always have to be in accordance with that greater purpose in life.

Rick says in his book that we are made to worship. Our purpose in life is to be defined by something greater than ourselves. In turn, that greater something empowers us to be fully alive. But the God of love who created this world has given us a choice of what we worship, of what we put our ultimate hope and trust in. That is, again, the lesson from Adam and Eve's test in the garden. We are independent contractors given this incredible task of building our lives, becoming mini temples of devotion. But however we stand or fall is based on the integrity of the temples we build. The Bible certainly makes that clear.

"Now devote your heart and soul to seeking the LORD your God. Begin to build the sanctuary of the LORD God, so that you may bring the ark of the covenant of the LORD and the sacred articles belonging to God into the temple that will be built for the Name of the LORD" (1 Chron. 22:19). From the Old Testament, these are King David's words to his son Solomon, who was entrusted with the sacred task of building the Lord's temple, which would serve as the nerve center of Israel's devotion to the Lord God. It was a physical sign that they would no longer be wandering exiles. They would be rooted in the land that God had given to them, his promise to Abraham, and that God himself would reside among them through the ark of the covenant, the container holding the stone tablets on which the Ten Commandments were written.

But there's a curious parallel here to another type of temple in the New Testament, as Jesus equated his own body with a temple. He said, "Destroy this temple, and I will raise it again in three days. . . . But the temple he had spoken of was his body" (John 2:19, 21).

If there is a coherent thread between the Old and New Testaments, which Christian theologians believe, then David's words can also be understood as instructions to us for how we build our own bodies and minds as temples of worship. It's really just a formula. First, there's the laying of a spiritual foundation, what we seek with all our hearts and souls. Then, seamlessly flowing out of this devotion, a covenant is created, a cornerstone of trust, of law and love comingling, setting the parameters for what is deemed good or bad, for how we judge the actions of others and ourselves; finally, the gathering of sacred items, things that enhance our worship.

All along the process choices are made. But it's the first choice that is the most important; it provides the spiritual foundation for every decision we make in life. Whoever we are or are not, is based on that foundation.

A TALE OF TWO FOUNDATIONS

A few years ago I covered a story in Buffalo, New York, about an artifact that had been discovered in the Catholic diocese there. But there was another story that proved even more fascinating. While talking with Bishop Edward U. Kmiec, I happened to see a large bell sitting on the front lawn of St. Joseph Cathedral. Usually church bells reside high above the ground in towers; hence the name bell tower. So I asked him, "Where did the bell come from, and why is it on the lawn?"

Bishop Kmiec said that the bell was from the tower of the new church. I asked, "New church! Are you building one? The one you have is pretty spectacular."

"No," he said, and went on to explain. The St. Joseph Cathedral now standing is actually the old church, completed in 1870 as a vision of Buffalo's first bishop, John Timon, and "as a great monument to our Savior."[1] But in 1902, Bishop James Quigley, the city's third bishop, decided Buffalo needed a new cathedral befitting the city's bustling growth as a hub of commerce and industry. So the new St. Joseph was built and completed in the year 1915. However, the new building couldn't take Buffalo's climate of extreme cold in the winter and sweltering heat in the summer, which exposed its structural frailties. Not long after it was built, it began to show its weaknesses and fall apart. It was in constant need of repairs. Finally, in 1977, the patching up became too costly and the new church was dismantled. All that was left was the bell.

The drama of these two cathedrals got me thinking about what could have been God's reasoning for allowing one building to stand and the other to fall apart. If all things happen because of God's providence, then what is the difference between these two structures? If it is because of frugality, meaning, "You don't need two churches," then perhaps it would have been better not to allow them to spend millions on a new structure in the first place.

Not finding a practical reason, I thought, *What's to be learned from this?* So I did a little research on the two cathedrals.

I found a certain incident in the old cathedral's early life that might be a clue. When the cathedral was being constructed, a treacherous storm blew in off of Lake Erie and destroyed many people's homes. Bishop Timon invited the people to find shelter within the walls of the cathedral under construction. I can only imagine the prayers said under those conditions by people who had lost all their worldly possessions. But in the shelter of the church, there was security and many a grateful heart. God's house of worship became a literal shelter in the storm.

Perhaps the new St. Joseph Cathedral was impressive looking. But despite its beauty, the architects ignored or never understood certain rules of climate, of stress and strain, and in a sense violated the natural laws, and by that they violated God's covenant governing architectural requirements. Regardless of what kind of building it is, unless certain rational, objective rules are followed, it cannot stand. This is the covenant of creation. All the natural laws are part and parcel of that legal contract, a divine contract where God alone sets the parameters.[2]

Covenants cannot be broken. They can, however, be superseded by other covenants. For instance, the discovery of lift could be viewed as a covenantal law of aerodynamic force that allows planes to fly. Without understanding its rules, we would not have air travel. The law of lift did not change the law of gravity. It is a law discovered *because* of gravity. Covenants, natural laws, can never be broken without serious penalties. His covenants, like his love, endure forever.

In Buffalo I saw the builders ignoring God's laws through either ignorance or arrogance. Either way, it caused them to make errors in the construction of the new cathedral. The old St. Joseph was dedicated to the Savior, and its first gift of practical help saved people from a terrible tempest storm. It is a lesson that is now always a part of the old church's legacy, one of its foundational stones, so to speak.

Bishop Timon had wanted a cathedral built to the Savior; he had made a covenant that the church would be built on that firm foundation of honoring the Savior. In being a physical shelter in a storm, the church would always carry that legacy spiritually as well.

It is unclear why Bishop Quigly was building the new church. Perhaps, like the biblical Tower of Babel, the new cathedral was ostensibly built to the glory of God, but God saw that it was really raised to the glory of man.

Finally I realized something less speculative and far more personally humbling. God was opening my eyes, showing me something about myself. The problem didn't just lay *out there*. It was also *in here*. *I* was the embodiment of the saga of those two cathedrals. I, too, at one time in my life relied on improper building materials and methods, ones that couldn't provide proper support, ones that couldn't weather the storms of life. I had failed to see my purpose in all that I did.

A Personal Lesson

This is a story about myself I've rarely shared, but I have now because I believe it will help others—what I did I'm sure millions of others have also done but through other means. I have been known for my success in pageants; I was Miss Minnesota and third runner-up in the Miss America Pageant. It's still very prominently featured on my résumé and bios. But what is not known is why I put so much energy into those competitions. At a critical point in my life, why was it was so easy to pour all of my creativity into gowns and crowns? When I broke up with my first boyfriend, the pain was awful. It was a searing, burning pain that no amount of crying and wailing seemed to assuage. But what gave me a sense of consolation was focusing on a pageant. It gave me a purpose and helped me find something to pour my life into, something that would give my ego a boost. Even if I lost, I was better for it. But what I didn't realize was that focusing on an exterior pursuit didn't allow God to help me make sense of the pain of a lost relationship. It didn't allow God to show me what I needed to learn about true love. I needed God to stand on, but instead, I used the personal goal of winning a pageant rather than learning how to pursue love in a healthy, giving way. It took me years to learn to love like that. And it took years to finally find a man I could marry.

This isn't a negative sentiment about pageants. I believe they are incredible opportunities for young women and I heartily recommend them. The personal growth is amazing. But pageants cannot be used as a source of love and acceptance. Love and acceptance come from God alone, not from exterior aggrandizement. I will always be proud of my pageant successes, plus many of the close friendships from those days I still have, more than thirty years later. And I learned a crucial life lesson: your fear of losing should never be greater than your desire to win. That is the emotional equivalent of being between a rock and a hard place. You can never win a pageant without letting go of your fear of losing one. You can never win at love unless you throw away your fear of being hurt. Both rely on knowing a greater love.

I, like many people, had built my life on surfaces of questionable integrity, committing myself to something that was not built for that purpose. A footbridge cannot handle the weight of a Mack truck. And a career, or a pageant, cannot handle the weight of your soul. Oh, there will be lessons learned, as with any pursuit. But all have to be weighed and measured in the context of who we truly are and who God is.

A SINFUL REALITY

When I tell people I'm the chief religion correspondent for Fox News, I sometimes get a lot of negative responses. A common one is that "religion is responsible for all the problems in the world; wars, tumult, hatred, and strife."

My response, if I choose to engage the person in conversation, is that religion essentially is the red herring, the thing that people focus on which is not really the problem. The real problem in the world, the cause behind the cause, is sin. And that is common to all people of all religions. This is the brokenness I explained earlier. But to engage people of various backgrounds, I usually leave out the Christian theological answer.

Now most of us understand the word *sin* as something that is bad, something that we ought not to do. But ask people to define it, and their answers can get a little hazy. It boils down to, "I know it when I see it." Which also means most of us look outward to find sin, rather than inward. It's so easy to see it in other people but so difficult to recognize it in ourselves.

I've heard some feel-good Christian preachers, who shall remain nameless, describe sin as "missing the mark." But that definition of sin misses the mark by a long shot.

Briefly said, sin is putting ourselves in the place of God. In architectural terms, sin prevents us from building ourselves into the temples God would have us be. Sin perverts our intended fixed point, which is the light of truth in God, and replaces it with a darkness that is less stable. Sin takes the covenant of the fixed point—the spiritual form of the Pythogorean theorem that creates the structural integrity of all buildings—and replaces it with something else that cannot shoulder the burden, cannot bear the responsibility of making sure the edifice will stand the test of time.

For physical buildings, and for us, there is no choice of whether to have a fixed point. There's only a choice of what that fixed point will be, of what we choose to make a covenant with. There is no default position of "no foundation, no fixed point." We must stand on something. If it is not God's Word, it is something else.

A False Foundation: A Tragic Loss

The news story of a ten-year-old New Jersey boy's tragic reaction to losing a board game broke my heart. I share it here because of how young the boy was. It shows that we can find our purpose in life during any life stage, not just when we're adults.

The report said that after losing a chess game to a fellow student, the boy jumped out his school's second-story window. He died a few hours later at the hospital from his injuries. Before he jumped he'd huddled in a corner of the room crying and wrote a note to the student who had bested him in the game. The note's contents were not disclosed. School authorities said the boy had battled depression. His fellow students who had played chess with him before said that he'd threatened to jump out a window as he began to lose.[3] What happened? Why did the boy react so violently to losing a simple chess game? Psychologists point to depression and mental illness. That certainly is part of how his real issue manifested itself.

But perhaps at the heart of why he became depressed is that he, unknown to himself, had made a covenant with winning. As I look at the boy's trauma from an outsider's point of view, it would seem that winning, or being the best, had become the boy's foundational purpose in life. And when he wasn't the best, when he got close to losing, or when he lost, his covenant had been violated, and the failure to live up to that purpose demanded that a penalty must be paid. His fear of losing was greater than his desire to win.

For some reason, unknown to me and perhaps to the people around him, the boy had bound himself to a belief that was not accurate, building himself into a temple and becoming high priest to its devotion. Its high altar, the fixed point. But it did not reflect the reality of the Master Architect's plan.

SEEING PURPOSE: A BLIND COOK'S FIXED POINT

The story of Christine Ha is quite different. She's an example of someone who suffered incredible hardship, but put her hopes in a greater purpose for her life. As a teenager, she was devastated by the death of her mother from cancer. But before her mother died (who was a Buddhist by birth) she began to believe in Jesus as her Lord and Savior. Christine began her journey of faith in Jesus at the same time, although at thirteen, the struggle was different. It took a few years before her faith became a living reality. She wrote, "By the grace of God, I not only survived it [her mother's death], I became a pillar of faith and a living testimony of how He makes all things possible."[4]

Years later, Christine's faith would be tested again. In 2004, at age twenty-five, she was diagnosed with neuromyelitis optica, an autoimmune disorder that caused her to lose her vision. Within three years she was virtually blind. But before she lost her sight, she found great joy in cooking; her specialty was Asian and American comfort food. Her talents earned her a spot on the reality cooking show *Master Chef*, the first blind contestant to ever appear on the program. She won. And now she has her own cooking show.

Christine's life example shows a faith in God's purpose for our lives, and she built her life accordingly. She wrote in 2006, "The cliché is true: God works in mysterious ways. Without challenges that stretch us, there is no growth or knowledge. With His mercy, greatness can come from hopelessness."[5]

Both Christine and the boy were living temples to what they believed their purposes in life were. One was false and ended in tragedy. The other was a true purpose, which even tragedy could not destroy.

Facades and Faith

Sometimes, however, facades create the appearance of a life of purpose and a foundational devotion to God. But facades of faith often mask the temple to a false god within. I had an encounter with one woman who not only lived out that reality in her own life, but came face-to-face with it in someone else in a way that humbled her and helped her realize that she had the awesome task of being an instrument of God's grace.

Sheila Walsh is a great woman of faith who is a talented singer, author, and speaker. She has an incredible testimony of finding strength through recognizing her own weaknesses. We met at a diner in New York City, and I was struck by her powerful presence. I also have to admit feeling a bit lacking next to her. She exuded such confidence, beauty, and charm. She's often asked to speak at church gatherings, to give other women encouragement. Over dinner, she shared that during one of her early speaking opportunities, she felt extremely inadequate. She said she didn't really feel qualified to talk about getting yourself together when she felt she had so much growing in faith yet to do.

She also said she didn't really feel that attractive, and on one of her appearances in a Southern state, she said she was intimidated by the Southern beauties in the audience who'd come to hear her speak. They were all decked out in their finest designer digs. She said one woman in particular in the audience was so beautiful she could hardly turn away. This woman looked like Miss America and a supermodel rolled into one: blond, tall, with a figure to envy. During the talk Sheila shared her testimony of God's love in the face of great turmoil in her life. Sheila truly opened up her heart, baring deep wounds that she had kept hidden from others and herself. She noticed that during her talk the beautiful woman was wiping away tears. Many women wept a bit, but it seemed odd to Sheila that that woman, who was probably the envy of many women there, would be weeping. After all, from the outside, she looked as though she had nothing to cry about.

Sheila's speech was well received and afterward many of the women came up to her. One of them was the extremely beautiful one. She told Sheila how much her talk meant to her. The woman then proceeded to show Sheila the scars on her arm she kept covered with clothes. The scars were from when she had attempted suicide. It hit Sheila like the proverbial ton of bricks. What Sheila thought about this woman from her outward appearance was a far cry from what was going on inside of her. There was turmoil, pain, and hurt. This woman was suffering, but no one could see it because her beauty was the facade they saw, and they made assessments according to what was on the outside.

Sheila said she felt ashamed at having judged the woman and knew that God was showing her something vital about these frail human structures. That more times than not, we spend most of our resources making covenants with what's on the outside. The covenant of beauty to project an image of having it all together, with a wall of makeup as brick and mortar, a fence of fashion as protection to let few see that our inner framework and structure is crumbling away as we desperately look for something to save us. In sharing this, Sheila helped me see in myself and in others that what is on the outside is not always an indication of what's on the inside. And no matter who I encounter, I must first see him or her as made in the image of God and work to connect with the spirit that needs, nay craves, to be close to that God. When the temples that we've built break down and crumble, the only hope for us is a renovation, one that is based on the Great Architect's original plans.

My Brother's Keeper: A Reliable Renovation

The older of my two brothers, Leslie, is one of the greatest men I know. He has a doctorate in education, was at one time the head of the Minnesota State Parole Board, and became the number one authority in the country on determinant sentencing for minority offenders. He was nominated to the United States Parole Commission by President Jimmy Carter but could not get on the agenda for Senate confirmation before Carter left office. He's on several boards in his community of St. Cloud, Minnesota, and his wisdom is constantly sought. He's been married to the same woman, his first and only wife Sally for nearly fifty years. They have four children and several grandchildren. He also walked me down the aisle for my wedding, standing in for my father who had died years before.

But growing up, I barely knew Leslie. First, because he is fifteen years older than I am, so by the time I knew who was who in the family, he was not living at home. And that brings up the second reason: he was in prison. From the time of my earliest recollection through the bulk of my elementary school years, Leslie was incarcerated. But I never thought about it because my parents never brought it up or obsessed about it in front of me.

But I think about it a lot more today, because how Leslie got from prison to upstanding citizen is a tale of loneliness, anger, love, hope, and redemption. It is a cautionary tale of what happens when we don't understand our ultimate purpose in life. When we make bad decisions our lives fall apart. But it is also a story of hope, of what happens when we allow a

God of grace to take charge of the renovations. We can have a life built on a firm foundation and a love that surpasses all understanding.

Leslie is the second oldest in a family of five children. He was a "very tall, knocked kneed, pigeon toed, and lanky"[6] teen, who felt he didn't quite fit in. His generation of teens grew up in the late forties and early fifties. He explains in his doctoral dissertation that, "My experience in high school of feeling inferior among white people and inferior among African Americans fed into my own story of hopelessness."[7]

There's so much more to Leslie's story than I can tell here. But the flyover narrative is that he got in with the wrong crowd, the supposed cool kids; and soon fell into drugs, alcohol, and stealing, the trifecta of bad-boy behavior. It was just a matter of time before he was arrested. He wound up behind bars and angry at my parents for not mortgaging the house to bail him out. My parents later talked about how hard that decision was, that they cried from the pain of their oldest son locked behind bars, asking themselves, "Where did we go wrong?" But they also knew that they had four other children to look after, including the two youngest little girls not yet in school. They couldn't sacrifice them because Leslie made some bad choices. Leslie, they decided, would have to pay the price for his crimes.

But Leslie was not left to stew behind bars alone. Like many a story of redemption, there may be several people who answer God's call to help one of his children come home. And that is the case for Leslie too. He talks about those people in his writings. But I can only tell of what I knew of him. Like the time my parents and I visited him in prison. I remember being about three years old and taking a long car ride, then finally arriving at a large gray building. I also vaguely remember black bars and Leslie sitting opposite my mother as we talked to him. He seemed in good spirits, but at my age, how was I to know? My first real recollection of my brother was that moment. Others in my extended family knew him so much better, and it was one of them who became Leslie's angel of mercy and made all the difference in his life, and who later made a huge impact on my life.

Our great-aunt Wreatha, or "Aunt Wreathie" as the family often called her, who would later teach my sister Lois and I about the game of Bunkum, wrote to Leslie while he was locked away. She didn't judge him. She encouraged him, gave him a glimpse of a better future. She sent him the famous book, *The Power of Positive Thinking*, by Norman Vincent Peale. The 1952 book was a trailblazing eye-opener about overcoming the problems of everyday life. Dr. Peale, the minister of one of the first megachurches, Marble Collegiate in New York City, was one of the first to combine religion and psychology, helping millions see a brighter future. It was the thing that transformed Leslie's thinking about who he was, who God is, what his purpose in life was, and how to build his life.

Leslie tells the story of how he just woke up one morning in his cell after reading the book with this awesome feeling that he was free. He realized that the only real prison in life was the one he built to a false god. That morning he said he looked at the prison guard, smiled broadly, and said, "Good morning! How ya doin'?!" The stunned guard didn't know what to think. Here was this young black man who was in prison, but acted as if he owned the world.

With God's guidance, Leslie has demolished the rickety life he was in the process of building, and instead let God help him build a better foundation and put his faith in God's abilities to guide the process. He lived out King David's instructions to his son, Solomon.

"Do not be afraid or discouraged, for the LORD God, my God, is with you. He will not fail you or forsake you until all the work for the service of the temple of the LORD is finished" (1 Chron. 28:20).

He could be honest about his life because he no longer feared it crumbling. He once told his students, "I was in jail not because I was black, but because I was a thief." Leslie had made a choice to trust in God. And that trust helped him build a better future.

This story is heartwarming because nothing in Leslie's environment was at fault. He had good parents, a good upbringing. He'd simply made bad choices. So the renovations were only a matter of hiring the right contractor, pulling the right permits, and obtaining the proper materials, which Dr. Peale's book opened Leslie's eyes to. His life from that point on would be now on God's Word, a firm foundation. He was lucky, we all were, to have Aunt Wreatha who helped guide our choices. And that brings up another point.

Sometimes, making conscious choices are not all that's at work in our lives. There are things that happen to us, that are done to us—for us and against us—that are a big part of who we are. They have great power over us, greater than we know or suspect. As we leave the topic of the covenant, it leads us to the second part of the story of our created world, the sacrifice.

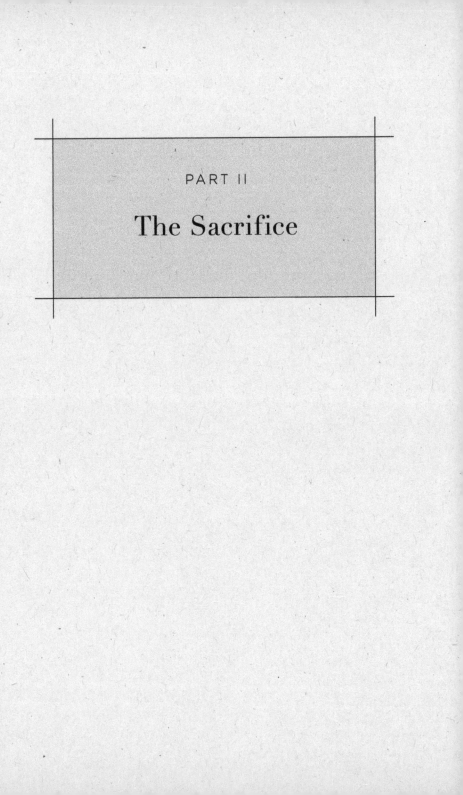

PART II

The Sacrifice

CHAPTER 5

The Tears,
the Blood, the Power

For as all die in Adam, so all will be made alive in Christ.

—1 CORINTHIANS 15:22 NRSV

THE COVENANT OF CREATION, I BELIEVE, HAS PLACED
the spark of "Let there be light" in us all. It's God's lamp, always within,
always near; a sure sign that God never abandoned us to be orphans or to
be without hope (John 14:18).

I also believe that that light in all of us longs to be joined with other
lights in a perfect union of love and harmony. But the light in us can only
be fully illuminated once we're bathed in the divine light of God's love.
It's the only love that can never be taken away, the only love that can fully
satisfy, and the only love that "surpasses knowledge" (Eph. 3:19). And we're
learning through our study of God's immutable laws that all other lights
become a shadow preventing the true Light from entering in. This causes
the bitterness that comes with our tears.

THE TEARS

While still in her teens, she married her first cousin, not unusual in the Muslim country of Morocco where she was born and raised. Young brides and multiple wives are all relatively normal. Her father had two wives and ten children between them. Laila was the youngest of them all, the last child of the second wife. Her cousin, Josh, was in his early twenties when the two married. Josh brought his new bride back to the United States, to Connecticut where he grew up. There, things were pretty nice for a while. He had a good job. She stayed home. Not too long after, she gave birth to her greatest joy, Alladin, a personable and jolly baby, the kind who everyone wants to hold and play with. So between a happy husband and a perfect child, life was wonderful.

But a little more than a year into the marriage, things began to go wrong. Josh drank too much and began having affairs. Tensions grew between them. Deciding to make a fresh start, they moved to the West Coast, to California. One of Laila's half sisters, Fahima, and her husband also moved to the Golden State. But the new environs proved no more satisfying. And the new start they'd hoped for didn't last. Josh began drinking heavily again and having more affairs. But one affair turned into a love relationship, and he told Laila he wanted a divorce. After tears and anger, she granted his wish. She didn't even ask for alimony. Her sister was also having problems in her marriage and decided she, too, would make a clean getaway. They both divorced their husbands, and their exes sent them packing on a Greyhound bus with their young sons to New York City. Both had few resources. Neither knew how she would support her family. Alladin was barely school age. Laila, in her early twenties, arrived in New York with fifty dollars to her name.

But thankfully their oldest sister, Lanika, an angel of goodwill by any standard, came to their rescue. She didn't make much money, but she was able to pay the needed money to rent one studio apartment the two women and their sons could share. Lanika said to them, "When you get jobs and get on your feet, you can pay me back."

After a few months Fahima found another man, got married, and moved out of the studio. So Laila and Alladin lived by themselves. She got work as a receptionist and supported them both. Alladin grew into a lively young boy. He loved wrestling with his cousins. He also loved climbing trees. "He was like a monkey," she said. He would climb anything. He wanted to be so many things growing up, including a Power Ranger. He also loved Christmas. It's a funny thing for a young Muslim boy to love Christmas. But when you grow up in New York City experiencing the brilliance of the Rockefeller Christmas Tree, the Christmas Spectacular at Radio City Music Hall, and all the city lit up with the festivities around Christmas, it's hard not to like the Christian holiday, especially when you get gifts. Laila says that Alladin would get a little Christmas tree and decorate it and give her presents. That was the little boy Alladin.

But as he entered his teen years, he began to talk about becoming a lawyer, of making enough money to support his mother. He said, "I'm going to buy you a house next to mine that you'll live in so I can visit you any time."

"Why can't I live with you?" Laila would ask him.

"What, am I crazy?! You and my wife, two women living in the same house! No."

Such was their relationship. He was the man in her life; she, the woman of his greatest devotion. He was her greatest gift, the one good to come from a painful and failed marriage.

On one particular rainy day in August when he was fifteen, Alladin and some friends were out playing as they usually did. Laila said she got a call from him saying he was hungry. She said, "Okay, well, I'm cooking dinner, so when you come home, you can eat."

But first he still wanted to hang out a bit more with his friends. They liked to climb the structure attached to a transportation substation in Astoria, Queens. She said they loved climbing it because from one high point they could see the skyline of Manhattan. They could see the soaring landscapes of progress and possibilities. It was a good place to dream about the future.

Laila recounted that not long after she got off the phone with Alladin, maybe just a half hour or so, a police officer called and said she had to come to the emergency room at a nearby hospital. Her son Alladin was there. Because she had just talked with Alladin, she was not terribly alarmed; concerned, yes. So she called a friend with a car to see about getting a ride to the hospital. Then the call came that sent her concern to alarm. The police called again, his voice sounded more urgent, saying, "Where are you?"

She and her friend found a cab and got to the ER.

It's a time in life that many people have faced, that call from the hospital, a diagnosis from the doctor, or a split-second decision that alters the course of your life forever. Such was the scene for Laila as she arrived at the emergency room. Police officers were all around, activity everywhere. Her knees began to buckle. The air seemed heavier, dense, and it was hard to breathe. Every breath felt like lead in her lungs. Laila knew something was terribly wrong. This was not a simple broken leg or arm where she would later go home with a smiling Alladin and a limb in a cast. No.

The doctors said Alladin and his friends had been climbing near a transformer. His jacket had gotten caught on something. He'd been electrocuted and was burned over 80 percent of his body. He fell to the ground, but the doctor assured her he felt no pain. He was still alive, but they needed her permission to transfer him to a trauma center that could better help him. That was why the police officer's call was so urgent. Alladin was barely alive and needed surgery if he was going to have any chance.

Laila called Josh in California. He immediately flew to New York. It was Josh who talked to the doctors about Alladin's condition. Laila was far too distraught.

The doctors amputated both Alladin's legs at the hip joint. But he still wasn't improving. The only other procedure would be to amputate part or both of his arms. The doctor said even then he would likely not survive. It was no use. Alladin, it was certain, would die.

"I just stopped like . . . like kind of stopped living," Laila told me through her tears. "I just got mad at God . . . at everything in my life."

"And then they said, 'There's no hope. No hope whatsoever.'"

With a barely audible voice, Laila said, "And they took him. They unplugged him."

At that moment Laila said, "I did not want to live. I just, I just didn't want to live anymore."

She said it wasn't as if she wanted to commit suicide. It was that she just wanted to lie down and never get up, to close her eyes and be in a better place. But life goes on. And the biological mechanisms that keep us alive are still at work even during tremendous tragedies and traumas. We cannot stop them. Life pushes forward; it must go on. It's like the old axiom that God gives us only what we can bear. And that which does not kill us makes us stronger. That is small comfort while you're in the hellhole of pain.

Even seven years later, as she told me the story of that day, Laila wept with fresh tears as if it had happened only a few weeks, or a few days, before. She said, "It wasn't fair. I was mad at everybody. I was mad at myself, at God because he took my . . . my only good thing!"

I asked her, "Did you ever get any answers about why [from God]?"

She shook her head.

I say to myself what anyone would say at hearing Laila's sad story, of anyone who believes in a loving God who allows things to happen for his own purposes. And that is, *God, how in the world could anything good come from this?*

And so, that's what I ask Laila. She is a Muslim, believing in one God, but not a God who has died for his image bearers. I ask her, "Can you see anything good that can come from this?"

There's an emphatic "No. Nothing good can come from this."

Alladin had become so strong a light in her life that God's light seemed only a dim flicker of a candle in comparison.

I so wanted to tell Laila of how I know that a good God would not leave her to suffer without hope, that the God I worship is a loving God who is there to comfort, and whose love endures forever.

But that is our dilemma, and certainly mine in trying to comfort a friend. To be faced with the Bible's description of a loving God, but then to be faced with the reality of pain and suffering. How can a loving God have allowed such a horror to happen to a single mother?

I could fill these pages with tragedy after tragedy, of people's lives altered and turned upside down from the pain and suffering they've endured. I think of my friend Sarah, who sits in the pew behind me at church, and who runs a ministry to help pregnant women after they've delivered a still-born. Their greatest joy became their greatest sorrow, as they deal with a personal pain few of us can understand. Sarah told me, "There are no answers, only questions. 'Why did this happen? What did I do to cause it? Who's responsible? Is God punishing me?'"

With every sorrow, the same questions: I think of a colleague of mine who was heartbroken about a promising young student at the high school where her kids attend, who was standing on a corner when a bus struck and killed him. I think of my brother's death from cancer, my father's too. We each have our stories, Laila's, a poignant and powerful example of one of the most heart-wrenchingly awful.

I didn't know what to say to Laila. I couldn't tell her what God's grand plan could be behind the death of her most precious son. I didn't know. But I did know one thing: that God also knew how she felt because his only son died, and something good did come from it. But how to explain that to a woman whose religious faith did not have a template for a resurrected Savior?

THE SOBER TRUTH

Death is the great equalizer. Its fate awaits us all. Kings, queens, peasants, or prophets, from great to small none of us can escape that destiny. It does not recognize religions, creeds, or races. And when it happens to people we know and love, it alters our perception of the future. Death has the ability to radically rearrange what we thought our lives were about. Wherever it happens, whenever it happens, death changes us. The closer relationship we have to it, the greater effect it has.

So I realized that death wasn't the real dilemma. It was how to process death, how to understand it in the context of what I believed to be the narrative of life in God's world.

But here I was, a Christian, listening to a Muslim woman's despair at the death of her only son, her only child. What was I to do? I knew that Jesus had died to save us. But I had no theological bridge to translate that into any wording that would help her. All I could think of at that moment was a gospel song that we'd sometimes sing in church: "The blood that gives me strength / From day to day / It will never lose its power."[1] Somehow I knew that these words held the answer, but how?

THE BLOOD

When I was young, the words, "There's power in the blood," were just lyrics in a song. But as I got older and life happened, the words became weapons of survival, because I needed strength on more than one occasion. I also knew that in order for me to make sense of it to Laila, and her pain, I could not just believe it for myself. I had to understand why, that no matter where we are in life, no matter who we are in this world, the power of the blood of Jesus Christ is light in a darkened world. Because blood also ties directly into the marriage of God's law with his love.

LIFE IN THE BLOOD

Blood is universal. All of us have it, animals too. It is a sign of life. Without blood rushing through the veins of creatures, there is no life. God said to the Israelites of old, "For the life of a creature is in the blood, and I have given it to you to make atonement for yourselves on the altar; it is the blood that makes atonement for one's life" (Lev. 17:11). These words were part of the Israelites' instructions of how to make animal sacrifices, a continual practice they were to do. The animal's blood was a substitute for their blood, a debt owed because of the original sin when man's ancient ancestor Adam, born to rule his world, instead bowed to Satan's lies and thus his authority.

By God's own edict, the wages of sin are death. Adam's actions allowed death entry into the world, allowing the great equalizer access to everything and everyone. But Adam's sin did something else, something far worse, if you can imagine that. It also severed his perfect relationship to God. The all-loving God must have been greatly grieved; because although he is love itself, by that very nature he is also judicious. Love creates boundaries. And so God allowed the transfer, which gave Satan ruling powers over earthly beings. But God never abandoned his favored creation; instead, he built within the world the means by which he would restore it and our relationship to Him.[2] The animal's blood was a mere shadow, a temporary substitute for the shed blood of Jesus Christ. His blood would be sufficient to pay the debt for all mankind, for all time. And Satan would finally be defeated. His lies and deceptions no longer would rule, because there's power in the blood of Jesus Christ.

But why is Jesus' blood treated so differently from ours? After all, Jesus was born of a woman.

THE BLOOD ON THE SHROUD

This astounding recollection may help explain. I once had an extraordinary yet personally challenging connection to the supposed blood of Jesus through an ancient artifact known as the shroud of Turin. It's a mystical piece of Christian culture, which is thought to be the burial cloth of Jesus. News stories about the shroud seem to generate more questions than answers. The persistent query is always about its authenticity.

There's a part of me that will always believe this is the cloth that Joseph of Arimathea wrapped around Jesus when he placed him in the tomb. But there's another part of me that is skeptical, that wants to withhold complete belief. I know because my own disbelief confronted me as I stared into the image of a replica of the cloth.

The replica is one of two commissioned in 1624 by Maria Maddalena of Austria, Grand Duchess of Tuscany, the wife of Cosimo de' Medici. It's not certain the whereabouts of the other replica, but the one now residing with the Dominican nuns of Our Lady of the Rosary in New Jersey is quite special.

The replica was such a good twin of the original that researchers in 1978 used it to practice on before working on the real shroud. In testing their equipment, they gingerly handled the duplicate as they would the original. Whatever they'd planned to do to the real shroud, they did with the replica. What made me gasp in wonder was when Sister Mary Catherine, the mistress of novices, told of how the replica, known as the True Copy, was made. The story goes that it had been placed on the original shroud. And at the spot of the side wound where Jesus was pierced with a Roman soldier's spear, the True Copy had spontaneously become damp as though with blood. Researchers confirmed it was blood on the replica. But that wasn't the most incredible part. What shook me to my bones was that Sr. Mary Catherine said the scientists discovered that the blood on the replica was the same blood that was on the shroud of Turin, from the same source! Now it could be the artisan who made the replica put someone's blood on both cloths. That certainly would explain why the two would have the same blood; unless the spot spontaneously became wet with blood without human intervention. But like the shroud itself, it is a mystery. And it is why the True Copy is venerated in the monastery.

The epilogue to my shroud encounter came as I looked through the dusty documents the sister had kept on file. I found a note from one of the observers, Edward Insinger, who had asked one of the main researchers, Dr. Alan Adler, to autograph the report on the shroud. "Dr. Adler," wrote Mr. Insinger, "signed it twofold: his autograph, followed by the structural display representing heme porphyrin, the major component of red blood cells found in all living matter—transporting oxygen from the lungs to body tissue. Upon observation of the heme porphyrin structural display sometime after the study, I was struck by the central portion, which I realized outlined the symbol of a cross."[3]

He went on to say, "The religious significance of the presence of a cross enforces the belief that we are studying a Cloth whose symbolism touches the very essence of the Christian faith—and all the people who pause to study and contemplate the Man of the Shroud."[4]

What the observer is struck by, and so was I, is that the chemical structure of the liquid that gives us all life has as its core shape a cross. What the Old Testament's book of Leviticus states, "the life of a creature is in the blood," science affirms in a way that is no coincidence. Our unique DNA, created at the moment of conception with that spark of "Let there be light," is present in our blood. And that blood's core element is shaped like the cross.

THE POWER

The question then becomes, "What is the major difference between Jesus' blood and our blood?" In our blood, yes, there is life. There's the oxygen and nutrients we need to survive, and proper regulatory mechanisms like waste management. But our blood is corruptible, meaning there's also the possibility of it succumbing to disease and death. For instance, leukemia is a cancer in the blood caused by a rapid production of abnormal white blood cells. Anemia is "tired blood," when there's not enough red blood cells.[5] Whatever is wrong or right with us, physically and biologically, is found in our blood.

But according to Scripture, Jesus' blood is incorruptible. There is no death, no disease. Only life.

Blood in the Bible, though, encompasses far more than its scientific qualities. It contains the soul of a creature. Mentioned some seven hundred times from Genesis to Revelation, blood is the single most prominent focus.[6] Moses proclaimed in Exodus, "This is the blood of the covenant" (24:8). God warned in Leviticus, "Neither shalt thou stand against the blood of thy neighbour" (19:16 KJV). In the New Testament there's a different tone about blood. It has power. The gospel writer John spoke of the "overcoming power of the blood."

Blood is practical and necessary, yes, but also a portent of a metaphysical and spiritual reality, containing the spirit of the person who communicates with God. After Cain slew Abel, God called him to account for the guilt of his brother's murder, saying, "What have you done? . . . Your brother's blood cries out to me from the ground" (Gen. 4:10).

The fearful side of God's message of the blood is his mandate that without the shedding of blood there is no forgiveness. Without something dying, losing the substance of its life, there cannot be atonement for sin. Because the Bible says the "wages of sin is death" (Rom. 6:23). Adam's sin was quite costly for us all. And that's why understanding how Jesus' blood is different from ours is nothing short of a revelation. It's what Scripture calls incorruptible. Jesus' blood is incorruptible. There is no death, no disease. Only life.

That blood is life is easy to digest. But that the shedding of it is tied to judgment is hard to swallow. How could a loving God, a God of love, allow for death as the only full requisite for forgiveness? And how could the *law* of a loving God lead to sacrificial death to atone for sins? Does this mean that Laila's son's death was a sacrifice to atone for his sins? Or even hers? It cannot be.

The Shedding of Blood

In answer to these questions, I later sought out one of the great theologians of our time, N. T. Wright. Dr. Wright is what you'd call an English intellectual; so incredibly knowledgeable, but quite affable and approachable, sort of like a character you'd find in an old Disney movie like *Mary Poppins* or *Pollyanna*. He's written thousands of pages on Christianity, especially the New Testament. He teaches at the University of St. Andrews in Scotland, famous now for two of its former students, Prince William and Kate Middleton, although he makes sure to tell people he wasn't teaching there when William and Kate attended.

Dr. Wright and I sat down to talk about the themes of this book and got on to this issue of the shedding of blood. It's important to understand, he said, that the shedding of blood is tied directly to this idea of sacrifice. And that sacrifice is tied to judgment, and ultimately for Christians, to forgiveness and redemption. But what's also important to understand is that sacrifice, particularly animal sacrifice, was not just in the Bible, it was universal to the human experience.

"You mean," I asked Dr. Wright, "sacrifice was not unknown to the ancient world?"

He answered emphatically, "Oh, no, no, no, very much the contrary. Everybody did sacrifice all the time, that's what you did. One of the problems for us today in communicating anything about the notion of sacrifice is that the vast majority of people in the Western world have never even seen an animal killed, let alone killed it themselves with their bare hands. . . . Let alone done it as an act of worship to a god.

"But in the ancient world that's what people did all the time. If you were going on a journey, you go to whichever god it was and offer a sacrifice. If your kids are getting married, you go and offer a few choice rams or bulls or sheep or whatever you could afford, to say to the god, 'Hope you're going to be on our side with this.' . . . Sacrifice was ubiquitous."[7]

I thought about this and concluded that if most all cultures sacrificed to gain some kind of benefits, it could mean that God, the real sovereign Being of the universe, had put in the hearts of all humanity the need for atonement, the inbred notion that something is wrong with us and that something must be sacrificed to make it right. Something must be given up in order for benefits to be received. And the most extreme form of that is death. It's as if the notion of sacrifice is a trace memory of Adam's curse in the garden, writ large and passed down to all of his descendants.

Unfortunately, without the knowledge of the true God, the ancient pagan cultures sacrificed not just animals but humans, particularly children. It was a well-known practice to sacrifice them to Moloch, which God condemned as the climax of their wickedness (Deut. 12:31; 18:10–13). I've included a chilling description below to show how heinous the ritual sacrifice.

The image of Moloch was a human figure with a bull's head and outstretched arms ready to receive the children destined for sacrifice. The image of metal was heated red hot by a fire kindled within, and the children laid on its arms rolled into the fiery pit below. In order to drown the cries of the victims, flutes were played, and drums were beaten; and mothers stood by without tears or sobs, to give the impression of the voluntary character of the offering.[8]

We are horrified that a culture would kill children to please a god, a false idol. But I'm not so sure modernity has shielded us from such evil. The sad reality is that children are abused every day. It was reported that in 2014 alone, 1,580 children died as a result of abuse and neglect. Also that same year nearly three quarters of a million children were victims of maltreatment.[9] Abused children could be considered modernity's form of child sacrifice. The question then becomes, "What idol is being appeased?" It is a question that deserves and needs a much longer answer than I can provide here.

But it is an example of how ubiquitous sacrifice is even today. In some shape or condition it is all around as a kind of ebb and flow, a giving and taking, a losing in order to gain, or a gaining that requires that someone else lose. In this way it is a fundamental truth of the world.

Our own bodies speak this truth. When we are conceived, the egg from our mothers and sperm from our fathers, which each carry a complete genetic code, must sacrifice some of those cells, some of that genetic information, in order to create a new human being. If they didn't, we might be born with four ears, eight legs, several eyes, and God knows how many multiple organs. After we've gotten a complete DNA and grow into a newborn baby, our cells must die in order to make way for new cells. Each knows to sacrifice itself in order for us to grow from fertilized egg to newborn, from child to teenager, and then to adult. This is a noble form of sacrifice that says, "My life for yours." The opposite of that is cancer. It is an evil that disrupts the ordered process of death to bring life. Cancer cells refuse to sacrifice themselves in order for the organism to grow. It is a biological form of Satan's lies because the cancer cells say to the healthy cells around it, "Your life for mine." It then demands that the host die, supplanting a healthy order for its destructive plan. In the end, by killing the host, it kills itself. That's the evil behind, "Your life for mine." It lives for today, for itself, not for the future.

THERE'S POWER IN THE BLOOD

But Dr. Wright's analogy of shed blood still didn't get to the answer of why Jesus' blood has such power. What is this power in the blood of Jesus? I was still floundering to find an answer, mulling over books and articles without getting one that satisfied. Until one Sunday I heard a fiery sermon delivered by a well-known pastor at a Baptist church in Harlem, New York. You could say this minister is a fire-and-brimstone kind of preacher. His words rang with passion, pathos, and truth. They were a revelation! The crescendo in his sermon uplifted me. And then he said the words that crystalized the message: "Oh! There's power in the blood!" Now he had my attention like I had never been focused before. He bellowed, "There's power in the blood to move mountains—to change whatever dire circumstance or condition in life. Because the power in the blood is the power of resurrection!"

Yes, the power to raise Jesus from the dead because death, Satan's curse, has no power over incorruptible blood. The great equalizer had not met its match, but its Superior. Jesus' blood is the incorruptible link to the power of creation, the power that said, "Let there be light."

A QUEST

My quest now was to make it understandable to Laila, a woman in pain, suffering the death of her son. So I extended my thoughts, reasoning that if Jesus' sacrifice on the cross is a truth for everyone, if all people put their faith in it, then I would hope to find evidence of sacrifice in the fabric and core of the world, the natural laws, not just in Christian theology. If this sacrifice is part of the loving God's plan, and that he, again, cast the net as wide as possible to take in as many people as possible into his redeeming arms, then I would expect that sacrifice is woven into existence itself, operating as a foundational principle of natural law and carved into the hard reality of the cosmos, present before the beginning of time. If the Son were present as part of the Trinity of the Godhead, as part of the love force that created the world, then his sacrifice on the cross would be an omnipresent truth that we could see, feel, and touch every day. Now it's time to look at the science of sacrifice, through what the Bible calls, "the blood of grapes" (Gen. 49:11).

CHAPTER 6

Lessons from the Vineyard

I am the true vine, and my Father is the gardener.

—John 15:1

The Vineyard

A rolling two-lane highway winds past what seems like countless vineyards on the North Fork of New York's Long Island. It is far less traveled than its South Fork twin, the Hamptons. While the South Fork is more prestigious and popular, the North Fork is more intimate and folksy. Its waterfront homes look over the snug Long Island Sound into Connecticut, instead of the panoramic vistas of the Atlantic Ocean. But because of its protection from the hurricane force winds that occasionally assault ocean-front land, it is the perfect environment for the bulk of Long Island's vineyards. Although they're not as well-known as the wine countries of France, Italy, or California, they still possess the same expertise for the ancient art of winemaking.

The same techniques have been known for millennia. The grapes make themselves into wine, fermenting forced by the sheer weight of grape upon grape as the volumes sit in vats crushing one another, forcing out their juices.

That's the first thing I learn from Peconic Winery's James Silver. Our talk began at around eleven on an April morning. At this time of the year the vines have neither leaves nor fruit. They appear as scraggly dead branches clinging to wires, as if grasping for their last chance at life. The only hint of hope for a future harvest are tiny round buds bubbling on the branches.

James is not a religious man and was a little scared when I told him I was writing a religious book. But I assured him that if he would talk about wines, God would help me see why the vineyard is one of his most powerful metaphors in the holy Scriptures. There's the sluggard in Proverbs who didn't give his vineyard the attention it needed and "thorns had come up everywhere, the ground was covered with weeds, and the stone wall was in ruins" (24:31). The state of the person's vineyard was the fate of his or her life in general.[1]

In the Song of Songs, the young woman in love refers to her body as her vineyard that she had not time to care for, but that it was hers to give away.[2]

The prophets Isaiah and Jeremiah both harshly criticize the leaders of Israel for failing to care for God's people who have ruined his vineyard (Isa. 3:14; Jer. 12:10). Isaiah's song of the vineyard expresses love for God and God's love for his vineyard, which is Israel, and his care for it as though he were a gardener who "cleared it of stones and planted it with the choicest vines" (Isa. 5:2). But, then he looked for a crop of good grapes, but it yielded only bad fruit (v. 4).

In the New Testament's gospel of Matthew, the vine and the vineyard became the source for Jesus' first miracle when he turned the water into wine at the wedding at Cana. It then became the source of one of Matthew's most poignant parables. He is the vine and we are the branches, and we must graft ourselves onto him for our salvation. The people of the vineyard became a metaphor for his church that he is establishing on earth: it's the parable of the workers in the vineyard. "Son, go and work today in the vineyard" (Matt. 21:28).

And then we see the climax of why the vineyard and the wine were not just metaphors as the wine became Jesus' most powerful resource at the Last Supper when it was transformed into his blood. He said to his disciples,

"This cup is the new covenant in my blood, which is poured out for you" (Luke 22:20).

But then at the end of time it represents the pounding reality of God's judgment on the people of the world: "The angel swung his sickle on the earth, gathered its grapes and threw them into the great winepress of God's wrath. They were trampled in the winepress outside the city, and blood flowed out of the press, rising as high as the horses' bridles for a distance of 1,600 stadia" (Rev. 14:19–20).

The theology of the vineyard, whether it's blessings or curses, is not too far removed from its biological reality. Certainly in an agrarian culture, vines and vineyards were visuals people could readily grasp. And because water was scarce, wine was more of a necessity.[3] But there is more.

LESSON ONE: TIME

My new friend James says people are a lot like vines in many ways. They live about as long as the average vine, seventy or eighty years. And they need time to develop fully. "Take the inland empire outside of Los Angeles . . . or the San Joaquin Valley in California, it's hot as blazes. Sure, if you irrigate it and put a great vine there, it would make a grape in two months. But it wouldn't taste like anything because it never developed physiologically. It never developed complexity, character. That's why they grow Thompson seedless raisins there. Because they don't need flavor and complexity."[4]

And that's so true with us. I knew a famous musician who had been a child prodigy and began his concert career at age seven. Although his talent never wavered as he got older, he grew into a narcissistic, selfish adult who had affair after affair. I happened to speak to a psychologist once about it to see if there was any connection. The psychologist said that with prodigies or any child with extraordinary gifts, their emotional maturity usually stops or slows once their careers begin. He said that we are relational beings who need time to go through stages of life. If you take a child out of that process, he rarely gains what he lost.

LESSON TWO: STRUGGLE

Another way we are like vines is that we both need to struggle. James says a vine "has to work hard. . . . It needs a balance of dry and wet, dry and wet, dry and wet."[5] There is no easy route for a vine. There is no sitting back and letting the vintner do all the work; a good grape needs to fight for its life. During drought, the vine's roots dig deeper into the soil to find water. Instead of watering the vines, the vintner essentially forces the roots to go deeper down to find the water table in the ground, to find its most abundant source of refreshment. Some vine roots are as much as twenty-five feet into the ground. It seems vines have a great deal more sense than people at times.

A friend of mine in my Bible study married a woman who was an atheist. A few years later they divorced. He became despondent and depressed and said that he had given up on God. I told him, "God has not given up on you." I also told him that the answer to his dilemma was not to abandon God but to go deeper into his faith. Don't look to be watered by temporary pleasures: another relationship, a higher paying job, a different place to live. The answer is to let your roots go deeper into the water table of God's love. God's Word assures us, "In this world you will have trouble. But take heart! I have overcome the world" (John 16:33).

LESSON THREE: PRUNING

Another lesson we can learn from the vineyard is that all vines must be pruned. James says that if vines are left to themselves, they will keep growing and growing, putting all their efforts into the growing of leaves. The vintner has to clip the leaves so the vine produces good fruit. James says vines seem almost grateful for being pruned, flourishing with abundant harvest.

We, on the other hand, don't see it as such a fine thing. Who of us rejoices in having his or her wings clipped? Years ago I auditioned for a musical group that I admired. I got pretty close to joining, was even invited to attend the summer workshop, which was the training ground for the touring group. At the end of the summer, I went home praying that I would get the call to join them. When the call came, it was to tell me that I hadn't made the group. It felt as if a dream had been cut away, wrenched from my life. But now I see it as God, the gentle Gardener, pruning away a superfluous branch from my life so that I could concentrate my energies on growing good fruit.

LESSON FOUR: WEEDS AND PESTILENCE

James says that only the gardener knows what can harm or destroy a vineyard. And weeds are troublesome. They'll grow anywhere, anytime, and under any kind of condition. If left alone, weeds will take over a vineyard or garden and steal the water and nutrients from the vines so that they cannot grow to their full potential. This is not the kind of struggle you want for a plant. But the vines cannot protect themselves against the weeds that can potentially choke them. The gardener must weed the vineyard as well as keep predators away like bugs, deer, and birds.

The more James talked about tending the vineyard, the more it seemed we were talking about people. In talking about the problem with weeds and pestilence in the vineyard, it felt like we were talking about sin and disorder in the human heart. "Sin is crouching at your door; it desires to have you" (Gen. 4:7).

Just as the default mode for a garden is weeds and wild plant growth, so, too, is the human spirit's, which is much like a garden, naturally inclined toward disorder, meaning an order away from God. Weeds don't need plant food or fertilizer to take over the garden. And children don't have to be taught to lie or challenge a parent's will. In both cases, it comes naturally. Weeds often grow faster and more easily than the desired foliage. So, too, does bad behavior among Adam's race.

THE VINEYARD'S LESSON OF SACRIFICE

The vineyard certainly serves as a powerful metaphor for our lives in relationship to God through Jesus Christ. But it also presents the compelling pattern for how living things, particularly seeds, grow. Seeds must die to themselves in order for a vine to grow. In other words, seeds must be sacrificed so that a new form of life can spring forward.

Let's go back to the beginning, when the world was created, to the covenant of creation. As you'll recall, the Big Bang was a hot mess. For there to be other elements besides those present at the beginning of creation, the hot mess had to cool. It had to give up its hotness; it had to yield being hot to bring forth a cooler state. And as you may recall, the first element to separate itself out after a slight cooling was gravity. Now scientists can look at this process and say, "That's how the natural world is." But if God created the world and devised the properties of all its elements, then the cooling process is also in his control. And the scientific word for that process is *entropy*.

ENTROPY

The law of entropy is the second law of thermodynamics, which says this: "In all energy exchanges . . . . if no energy enters or leaves the system . . . the potential energy of the final state will always be less than the potential energy of the initial state."[6] This is a scientific explanation that can make your head spin, and something to memorize for a quiz but not really to understand what it means. Let me explain a bit further.

The law of entropy means that things naturally cool down; they naturally dissipate; they die. For example, if I leave a hot cup of coffee on the table and come back to it in twenty minutes, it will no longer be hot. It can only be hot again if I reheat it, i.e. put energy into it to change its cooled state. We don't think of the coffee as dying, but what we can say is that the thing that gave it its hotness left, and it can't get hot again unless something outside of it gives it hotness.

Entropy, for scientists, is looked at as part of disorder, that things naturally decay from order to disorder. But I believe entropy is very much a part of an orderly world included in God's creation that he called "good."[7] "The flow of energy in living cells maintains order and life. . . . Entropy wins when organisms cease to take in energy and die."[8] From a scientific point of view, if this second law of thermodynamics, entropy, had not been in effect from the first moment of creation, and still around today, the cosmos would be devoid of stars, planets, and moons. It would be a cosmos devoid of physical life.[9]

Entropy is the pall of death and decay that hovers over and through the entire created order. But it is harmless in that it does not purposefully kill or maim or cause ill will. Rather, it is a vital and necessary element for the perpetuation of life. There is no life without death. There are no nutrients in the soil without something dying. Fossil fuels, part of billions of years of geologic history, testify to the process of the death of microbes and other organisms that created the existence of limestone, marble, coal, oil, gas, kerogen, peat, coral reefs, and guano deposits in great abundance on earth. They represent millions of generations of past life and death.[10] Life that ended so that other life could begin the cycle anew.

This is sacrifice that is part of God's orderly physical universe. This is the organic world where things grow and change because of this law of sacrifice. It would be simple to keep the law of entropy and sacrifice separate. One is an established physical law, the other more of an interpretation using the realms of philosophy and religion. But just like the rainbow, which God used to make a covenant with Noah, the law of entropy, also known as sacrifice, is part of the tool chest of God's redemptive actions. His law is all inclusive and his love flows through these natural laws. When Jesus died on the cross and was resurrected, God wasn't creating a whole new line of credit. He was using what was already at his disposal, what was present at the beginning of creation. God went into his storehouse, his stockroom, using what was already available to him in its raw, almost benign form.

THE GREATEST LESSON

Perhaps the greatest lesson from the vineyard is found in a word that is well known to wine connoisseurs but not as much to the general public. It's a French word called *terroir*. It's pronounced *tare-wah*.

My vineyard guide, James, says the whole term is *gout de terroir*. It's a phrase that literally means, "taste of the earth." It means the life each wine has lived through the climate it has experienced and the soil from which it has grown.

"We're talking about all the conditions that make a Chardonnay from California different from a Chardonnay grown in France. They're both Chardonnay, but they have lived very different lives."[11]

In short, *terroir* is the combined experience of the vines that produce the grapes that make the wine. Every season of its life, every struggle, every storm, every joy or sorrow, is its *terroir*. Now there's no doubt in my mind that we are vines living in God's vineyard. And our *terroir* is every experience, good or bad, that has made us who we are.

For now I must leave the vineyard and venture into the research labs and halls of academia to understand better what makes our human *terroir*.

Our *Terroir*

My first stop was at New York University to talk with Dr. David Tukey, a post-doctoral fellow in molecular neurobiology at NYU Medical Center. He was conducting groundbreaking research on the brain and obesity.

His basic work helps explain exactly how our *terroir* is created, by looking at how synapses in the brain change with experience.

Synapses are electrical "connections between nerve cells." There are trillions in our brains, forming a complex and flexible network that allows us to feel, behave, and think. Every move we make, every action, every thought has formed our synaptic connections. And the synaptic connections then get reinforced if certain actions are repeated. Synaptic connections are the wonderful things that allow babies to recognize faces, toddlers to learn to walk and tie their shoes. It's also what helps us learn to read, skip, ride a bike, and play music.

Dr. Tukey said, "Anything we learn . . . there's a physical change in the brain that accompanies that, that allows us to store information and develop new behaviors over time."[12]

And that's how our *terroir* is created. We come into this world with an endless amount of possibilities.

THE BRAIN

One who knows that well is Dr. Andrew Newberg, a neuroscientist who conducted a lot of research on the brain and faith.

Dr. Newberg and I sat down and talked in his office in Philadelphia where he researches and teaches. We talked over this idea of nurturing and the importance of life experiences. He said, "On a very fundamental level, the brain is able to grow and adapt, modify itself, change itself based on its environment."[13]

He explained to me how it works in young children, using the example of one simple mathematical problem.

Dr. Newberg said, "You have neurons in your brain that tell you one plus one equals two. And you have connections that tell you one plus one equals three, and one plus one equals four. But when you are told by a parent that one plus one equals two, then the one that tells you one plus one equals three (and all the other wrong ones), those connections start to go away. They get pruned away."

Another way of putting it is those synaptic connections that could keep telling you the wrong answer have no energy reinforcing them. So they die. It's a psychological form of the law of entropy at work. The connections that get reinforced get locked in your brain. But the crucial part here is that any thought, any mode of behavior has the potential to get locked in the brain through these growing synaptic connections and neurons.

I told him that this sounded like the negative form of what the Proverbs writer said, "Train up a child in the way he should go: and when he is old, he will not depart from it" (Prov. 22:6 KJV).

Dr. Newberg said, "Oh yeah, absolutely!"

GENES AND THE BODY

My next stop was across the pond to jolly old England. There I met with Dr. Denis Alexander. He's the head of the Faraday Institute for the Study of Science and Religion based in Cambridge University. Cambridge has incredible historical scientific significance. It is where scientists first split the atom at Cavendish laboratory in 1932. It's also where James Watson and Francis Crick in 1953 discovered the structure of DNA, the building blocks for all living things: plants, animals, and, of course, humans made in the image of God.

I first met Dr. Alexander a few years before when I was a Templeton Cambridge fellow, a program designed for journalists researching in the areas of science and religion. He is a biologist and a person of faith. He told me during the interview something that really will change the way we understand our *terroir*. He said we will no longer have the narrative that genes control our destiny.

Instead, he said, "There's a continual flow between our relationships, our interactions with people." Dr. Alexander said our minds are "constructed by our own relationships. Our own interactions with other minds."[14]

He continued, saying that the interactions begin from the moment we are conceived. Here's how the genes and the environment begin their relationship even in the womb.

"When you look at the development of the human organism, what you see first of all is you need the proteins to switch on the genes. . . . When you get a fertilization of the egg and you get the very, very early embryo . . . at that stage, the very first cell division, it's the proteins from the egg from the mother, which is actually beginning to switch genes off and on in that emerging tiny little embryo.

"So now, is that the environment? Or is that the genes? And immediately you start asking the question; you realize it doesn't mean anything actually, because it's like an orchestra, if you want to use a musical analogy. The genes are, if you like, just the instruments in an orchestra. Unless people are there to play them, they just won't give any musical notes out. So the genes are always in interaction with the cell and the contents of the cell, which means the proteins. There's always an interplay going on . . . and that happens right at the beginning of human development.

"In other words, what's emerging is, the way that the human being develops all the way through nine months of development in the uterus is a completely interactive symphony. There are so many factors playing the music of the genes. . . . And so, in other words, when you're saying, 'Well, what's in the genes? What's in the environment?' What are we actually asking here? We're actually asking a rather artificial question, because in fact . . . it's a system. It's the system that's developing."[15]

It is our *terroir*.

Dr. Alexander and his team at Cambridge explained that even identical twins separated at birth show differences in their *terroir*. Here's why.

"The first thing we notice is they're often not separated at birth," he said, a key point. "They're separated at three months, or they're separated at six months, or they're separated at nine months . . . then placed with adoption agencies. So they share the same uterus, often . . . they share the same placenta. There are other identical twins that have two different placentas. That makes a difference. They're always competing for the mother's nutrition. So there's competition going on between twins in the womb. One twin may well come out smaller than the other. They may not be bathed in the womb with the exact same levels of hormones, for example."[16]

A huge amount of synaptic development—this is what Dr. Tukey researched—is going on even in the first few months of life. The baby's brain at birth, said Dr. Alexander, is 20 percent of the final weight and size of the adult brain. But already at age five the brain of the young developing child will be at 80 percent of the adult.

Wow! It means from birth to age five is the period of time when our brains grow the most they will ever grow in our lifetimes. If you even ponder who you are and why you are the way you are, those early years of life have maximum impact because they have had the greatest influence on how we reacted to the environment around us.

"What happens at those times is really crucial, really crucial," said

Dr. Alexander, saying the words twice so I got the impact. "And of course we know from many animal studies and very sadly from some human [studies], that if they face neglect during those crucial early years of life, then their actual synaptic load is far less. They are deprived for life."

But hold on for a minute. I asked Dr. Alexander about this amazing ability in the human brain called plasticity. Because of the brain's ability to mold and be molded as we grow, doesn't that help to thwart whatever negative impact that may occur because of those early years?

"Not if they have serious neglect."

You see, Dr. Alexander explained to me something I had never heard of before about genes and DNA. It's something called *epigenetics*. He said the epigenome is another layer above that switches genes on and off.[17] That layer is plastic. But even though it is pliable, it, too, can be long lasting, like our cells and all the tissues of our bodies.

"You know we have 220 different tissues in our bodies. And the reason they're all different is not because they're different DNA in every cell of our body, because we have the same DNA in every cell of our body. Every cell in our body has the potential to be any other cell in our body. But epigenetic mechanisms switch off a panoply of genes and switch on a panoply of other genes; that's what makes a skin cell a skin cell or a brain cell a brain cell or whatever it is."

And the epigenetic switch is pretty stable. So once a skin cell is a skin cell, that's going to stay that way the rest of your life.

"So the epigenetic modifications in the cells that renew our skin, they're all kind of fixed. You know, if they weren't fixed you'd suddenly find brain cells growing on your head, which would not be good."

But there's something else happening in this biological interplay of genes and the environment. It's a sort of chicken-versus-the-egg syndrome. What came first? In this case it's a bit confusing. "DNA is under the control of proteins, which in turn tell the DNA what to do. But the DNA makes the proteins. DNA is making the proteins, and the proteins then are regulating the DNA."

Needless to say, I'm quite confused at this point, because if proteins turn the genes on or off at the beginning of life and throughout life on this epigenetic level, how does it all fit together?

He answered: "Well, it is like a recipe in a sense. It's a recipe for cakes, and cake can come out different every time. It's a recipe in the sense you take the DNA recipe, but . . . someone's got to make the cake. In other words . . . it's really the system that builds the body over a long period of time. It's a process, and that process is where you have a complex system, which is genes, proteins interacting with the rest of the environment. The environment means the cellular environment, the tissue environment, the actual . . . general body environment, and then the body interaction with the sort of external environment.

"So here's an example. Let's say there's an astronomer looking at the night sky, thinking, *Wow, isn't that amazing?* And there are epigenetic modifications going on in his DNA, *ch, ch, ch* . . . all the way down, because he went out at night and had a wonderful experience. And that might very well change his DNA in its expression. There is communication going on all the time. DNA is not static. DNA is always in motion, things are going on all the time."[18]

I'm totally blown away, because what Dr. Alexander is telling me is exactly what one doctor once expressed to me: that "our genes may load the gun, but the environment pulls the trigger."[19]

But then how much control do we really have? We don't choose what vineyard we're planted in. We don't choose our parents, our race, our cultures. We don't choose what time of year we are born or our physical characteristics, whether we're tall, short, have curly hair or straight hair, blond and blue eyed or brunette with dark eyes. And yet all of those qualities can profoundly affect how the environment around us nurtures us.

And what about free will and personal responsibility? From the way Dr. Alexander explained it, whoever we are, our *terroir* was made by life's many twists and turns.

BACK TO THE VINEYARD

As I return to the folded fields of vines at Peconic Bay, I now see more than the grapes that make reds or whites, rosés or Chardonnays. I comprehend the reality of living. We don't live life in theory, as if in a sterile classroom. Just like these vines in the vineyard, life itself is experience—pain and sorrow are not concepts, they are penetrating realities, forces that shape and mold us, break us, shatter us, and then bind us irrevocably to one another.

From the moment we are conceived, we are in a relationship, a relationship of constant give and take, food and growth, lack and prosperity, death and life. It's a complement of opposing forces, the yin and yang of existential creation. There is not a moment when our lives are not in this flux. Even the workings of our bodies is an intricate dance of organs, and cells, and sinew, all depending on one another for the survival of the whole.

God's laws are once again in play, both in our bodies and in the environment around us. We are affected by these laws in the personal decisions we make every day and most certainly by the decisions that others are making around us. They all affect the proper working of the mechanism we call life. We are on a constant journey traveling between feast and famine. When we are satiated, we begin the process of journeying toward hunger. When we hunger, we strive to be fed. Rarely is contentment experienced, unless the real hunger and thirst, the real longings underneath all the temporal longings and hunger, are satisfied. And that real hunger is not food. It is not physical matter. The true desire that powers the whole mechanistic system is love. Love. We have journeyed once again to an understanding that at the base of God's law is love. Love is what we're made for. Seeking it, having it, giving it. And Jesus' own words tell us how this love is the *terroir* we were meant for: "I am the vine; you are the branches. If you remain in me and I in you, you will bear much fruit; apart from me you can do nothing" (John 15:5).

So we try. For it is in love that we understand the sacrificial nature of living.

CHAPTER 7

Love Language and Sacrifice

I had planted you like a choice vine of sound and reliable stock.
How then did you turn against me into a corrupt, wild vine?

—JEREMIAH 2:21

THE STORY OF LOVE

With my mind and heart set on understanding love, the love that made the world, I was compelled to linger in the vineyard a bit longer. It was so beautiful, so satisfying. Here it was effortless to ponder the magnitude of love, resting in this garden, the garden of the blood of the grapes. I imagined God the great Gardener walking in the cool of the day through the even rows of vines; his love, rays of warm light, penetrating the deep soil, bathing even its darkest recesses. Here my thoughts about love grow, letting me feel its abiding nature; how the cycle of life and death and life again is nurtured in the soil of love's constancy. To love is to live. To live is to love. And to love anything is to risk pain and heartache. We ourselves are part of the medley and mixture of God's divine orchard, his creation.

In a perfect world, we are born because of the love of Mother and

Father coming together as one flesh. Their love creates new life. And at the moment that life is created, the moment of conception, there is that spark, that electrifying moment, a recapitulation of God's finest hour of creation's birth when he proclaimed, "Let there be light."

In that perfect world we would grow under the self-giving love of our mothers and fathers, who would nurture our needs and give us the sustenance of mind, body, and spirit to grow and mature, so that we, too, could repeat the cycle. All of this would take place to the glory of God—under his ever-present and always acknowledged love as Creator, Sustainer, and Breath of Life; our community would be a living testament to his love. And our hymn to him, "The love that made us, makes us one."[1]

That is love's original story in the garden of Eden. Perhaps it was part vineyard, with all its flowing fauna and fruits. But regardless, that story did not last. A pestilence in the garden perverted our love relationship with God, and by chain reaction, with one another. Our love of self became more important than love of God so that now love could not function in its purest form. The boundaries became blurred between love and lust, devotion and deceit, harmony and hate. Oh, we try to give it our best, strive to recreate our own little gardens of love. And some get close. But without seeking first the light of love at its source, we are bound to mess things up. And just as the Scriptures say, "In your [God's] light we see light" (Ps. 36:9). So it is with love, through his love we are able to love. His light is the "fountain of life" (v. 9), the wellspring of love.

MODERN-DAY VERSION

A few years back I took a self-help course in New York City. A coworker suggested it would be a transforming experience. It was a secular organization, and it was transforming, although not in the way the coworker might have thought. It helped me see that the Bible's redemptive story was the story. But I do believe that God uses even the secular elements of this world to direct us toward him. After all, as we've established already, it's all God's world.

There is one major revelation that I got from the course. And it's something that helped explain a traumatic childhood event. I should rephrase that. It was traumatic at the time. To the people around me, it was just another of life's little speed bumps.

The teacher of the course explained that when we are born we go along doing what little humans do. We're fed, our diapers are changed, and soon we learn to walk and talk and recognize the people and world around us. And life is our playful garden. Then one day, usually between the ages of four and eight, something happens to us, some event that shows us, nay, instills in our psyches, forever imprinted on our synaptic landscapes, that life is dangerous, that even the people closest to us cannot fully be trusted.

Most everyone has something in his or her background that he or she could recall. My event happened when I was six years old. I distinctly remember every detail of how I felt, what I thought, and what was said. To this day I still feel the pain that event caused, the churning in my stomach, the swirling in my head. It was in my first grade classroom at Horace Mann Elementary School. The boys in the class were being typically disruptive. And this time some of the other normally nice children were joining in. I, of course, was silent with my hands folded on my desk, as we were told. Mrs. Peters, our teacher, probably had had enough. Instead of picking out a few bad kids and naming names, she announced that the whole class would have to stay after school. I couldn't believe the injustice! How could you convict an entire class? I did nothing wrong. Then my six-year-old mind started to think, *I may never see my mom again! I'll never see my family again!* I looked up at the classroom windows and they looked like prison bars. And so I began to cry at my desk.

But this wasn't the worst of the experience. When we finally were allowed to leave, which I'm sure wasn't more than five or ten minutes later than school, as we walked home, my best friend at the time made fun of me, calling me Baby Huey,[2] because of my weeping. The cut went deep. But it would get deeper when I got home. My mother thought I had purposely dawdled after school and was angry at me. She yelled at me as I ran up the stairs crying, traumatized because I had wanted her to make it all better.

Instead she made it worse. I blurted out through my sobs and hiccups that we had to stay after school. My mother, instead of wrapping me in her arms and soothing my pain, went back to whatever she was doing. I was left to whimper alone. I remember hearing my older brother Kenny in the background, who was about twelve at the time, laughingly recalling, "Oh, I remember when my class had to stay after school!"

Now knowing my mother as a person and not just as my parent, I realize that she was not angry as much as she was scared. I was the youngest of five. My sister Lois and I always arrived home from school within a few minutes if not seconds of each other. That I was even five minutes late probably sent her into a tailspin of anguish. She probably imagined that the worst had happened. And the worst in the 1960s was a child getting hit by a car walking home from school. My mother's fears became my childhood trauma. For the next few years at school, I would begin to cry toward the end of the day if we were getting our coats on or preparing to leave before the bell rang. And later, it also became a reason I began to do everything in my power to hold back the tears so no one could make fun of me.

As I look back on that, I wonder if what I experienced was my own little garden of Eden fall-from-grace moment. Instead of enjoying the bucolic greenery and idyllic pleasures of being the object of my mother's love, pride, and joy, I was now cautious of all relationships. Only loving can cause this kind of pain.

What Is Love?

As I recall the landscape of my life's hills and valleys, I can say with honestly that love has been the sole shaping mechanism. In seeking it, holding on to it, or even repelling it, love has molded me into what I am today. And throughout my life I have been blessed by the grace of God to be enlightened by many—friends, family, and experts alike—who've had a profound impact on me as I've tried and strived to understand the nature of love: where it comes from, what effects it has on us, and why we need it so desperately. One of the most powerful examples has been the most recent. It's a sermon by my own pastor, Dr. Timothy Keller, based on the apostle Paul's letter to the Corinthians. It's the famous set of verses most of us hear at weddings, "Love is patient; love is kind; love is not envious or boastful or arrogant or rude" (1 Cor. 13:4–5 NRSV). And its most celebrated conclusion, "And now these three remain: faith, hope and love. But the greatest of these is love" (v. 13).

The first thing Dr. Keller said about this passage was that Paul did not have images of earthly nuptials in mind when he wrote these words. No. Paul was taking love to its bare bones, stripping away all the fluff of what we think about love and letting us see the active verb after the word *love*: *is*. What Paul was doing was personifying love, showing us that "love is a person who's like this . . ."[3]

Paul, he said, was trying to tell us that "love is not a set of abstract principles that you pick up and do. Love is an active power."

And like all power, it has a power source. And that power source is a person. "Before love is something you do, it's someone you meet."

He gave the example of why babies need to be nurtured with abundant love and held frequently. It's not just for the benefit of the parent. It's mostly for the baby. Babies learn to love by being loved.

"Love," he said, "is never something you do through trying, it is only something that happens if someone has loved you. Or put it this way, before love is something you do, it's a person you meet."

Because we can only give what we've been given, Dr. Keller said, "Love is not something you can generate, it's only something you reflect. The more love you have, the more love you're able to do, simple as that. If you're not bathed in love, you'll never be able to love, no matter how hard you try."[4]

"No branch can bear fruit by itself; it must remain in the vine" (John 15:4).

Just as the vineyard's vines are bathed in love's light and warmth, so, too, it must be with us.

"And if love is not something that fills up the deepest recesses of your heart, that you really feel and experience that love, everything you do morally is going to be actually using other people to fill that emptiness so that you can feel good about yourself. You won't be doing anything out of love; you'll be doing it for you."[5]

But the million-dollar question Dr. Keller posed in the sermon was, "Where do you get this kind of love?" If love is a person, then who is the person who has that kind of love that everyone on the face of the world, past, present, and future, can tap into? That kind of love cannot possibly be found in a parent, a lover, a friend, or even a child.

Theologically, the direct and short answer is that only God through the person of Jesus Christ generates that kind of love; that supernatural and divine love, which surpasses all understanding. But to be transformed by that love requires a far more circuitous route. As I have experienced.

My Love Fantasy

"He cuts off every branch in me that bears no fruit" (John 15: 2).

I am happily married now, but it was never the marriage I had always dreamed about; my husband is wonderful, don't get me wrong. And I thank God continually that I've been blessed to have this man as my partner in life.

But when I was a child, I had grafted myself onto the dream of getting married in my early twenties and having at least six or seven children; I even picked out names for them. I fantasized about having a nice house with a large yard and a garden of beautiful flowers and greenery. My husband would work all day, and when he came home, we'd sit around a big table for dinner. The children would then all have their baths and get tucked into bed. The day over, my husband and I would sit for a while by the fireplace, talking about the day, everyone's challenges, struggles, and victories.

Well, that didn't happen. And in my younger years there were heartbreaks, many of them. Now I see that they are all part and parcel of looking for love, as the song says, in all the wrong places—through people as well as achievements. But thankfully, and most blessedly, God used those experiences to nurture my better nature. Every heartache from a love lost was a seed planted: the pain, the Gardener's furrowing of my soul's soil; my tears, its nourishing water. The seed being sown, dying to its seed nature, coming to life as new creation. Throughout it all, God's loving light, providing the photosynthesis for a transformed and energized nature.

The Search for Love

I mentioned in chapter 4, in my younger years I competed in pageants, some of the best learning experiences of my life, especially that lesson of your fear of losing should never be greater than your desire to win, which I describe as the emotional equivalent of being between a rock and a hard place. I wanted to win, because it would be affirmation of something I had felt was lacking. I was never aware of my true motivation until later in life. But I got a hint of it in the first contest I entered: a teen pageant, with 152 contestants. I didn't win, and there were plenty of others to commiserate with, so the blow was minimal.

But the next pageant was a bit more exclusive, a pageant for high school seniors called Junior Miss. This time the odds were far better, a field of twenty-four contestants. I actually let myself imagine winning.

We spent a week in Owatonna, Minnesota, learning our choreography and rehearsing our talents and evening-gown positions. I'd sewn most of my competition outfits and to this day I cringe when I look at the pictures: *awful* is the only accurate description of the array of gaudy prints, inappropriate styles and fabrics, and generally bad-fitting garments.

For my talent I played a piano piece I composed called "Memories," a decent piece but amateurish now that I look back on it. However, it was good enough to help me make the top ten. What a feat! I was on my way to a state title. I knew I could do it. Well, I didn't. And my ego suffered a terrible blow, and the tears flowed. I pulled myself together enough to get to my room at the end of the night, and then I yelled and screamed, facing the wall. I tried to mute my wails with a pillow over my face so no one would hear. But even without the sobbing sound effects, my host mother knew I was in pain. The next morning she came down to my room with a glass of orange juice to give me words of comfort. What a good soul she was. She told me, "I know how disappointed you were at not winning."

I couldn't confide in her and admit the truth of what she said. I still remember her face, the small glass of orange juice, and the gentle words breaking through my hard defenses. I swore at that moment I would never enter another pageant. I would never make myself that vulnerable again.

But nearly two years later, I did. However, it took me decades to understand why. Why, after such a devastating loss, and vowing never to subject myself to such vulnerability, did I do exactly what I had vowed not to? The answer came years later. And what I now know is that I had sought pageants to affirm that I was loved, that I was worthy of being loved. But I was so loved, and I knew that even more as my host mother showed me more love in those brief moments than anyone outside my family had ever showed me, or that I had ever felt.

After not winning what I had so desperately wanted, it felt like I was dying. And part of me was. But it was a part I didn't need. Through that first devastating loss, God pruned the part of me that was afraid of losing. And what grew out of that death, in its place, was a stronger, more viable vine, nourished by the loving words of my host mother, but also by a greater, more ethereal love I had yet to fully understand.

The vineyard once more yields more than just its fruit. It's giving me insights into how we learn to love. We are bathed in a lingua franca of various dialects.

LOVE AS A LANGUAGE

As Dr. Keller said in a sermon, love is something we reflect, not generate. Our homes, the parents who brought us into this world, this is where we first learn about love. When we are babies, we can't name it or choose it, but we need it like we need air, water, and nutrients. We learn to love much like we learn to speak a language. We don't come into this world speaking English, German, French, or Portuguese. But we are born with all the tools needed to learn any of them. And we aren't born with a Southern drawl, or a

Cockney accent; we also get syntax, verb conjugations, and word meanings from those who are speaking around us. We can only reflect that speech. We cannot create a language unto ourselves. We learn the language to communicate with the people we are closest to. Language is about relationships.

And love is the strongest language there is, its communicative powers convey so much more than raw emotion. And it is learned much like we learn a spoken language. And just like language, we come into the world with all the tools we need to learn how to love. Read the following excerpt from a book on language acquisition; it could easily describe the way we learn to love:

> First, language acquisition is effortless. It involves no energy, no work. All
> an acquirer has to do is understand messages. Second, language acquisition
> is involuntary. Given comprehensible input and a lack of affective barri-
> ers . . . language acquisition will take place. The acquirer has no choice.[6]

Ah, that's the rub, the acquirer has no choice. We are born to love. Yet we must first be taught how to love. And our love skills are being taught to us before we even realize what's being taught. We're just helpless babies crying for our needs to be met. Does a newborn know he needs love?

And love, just like any language, is acquired as we grow, relying on what's around us as contingent beings. I am the daughter of, the sister of, the wife of. I am a student of school A, B, or C. I am a resident of . . . , I was born in . . . , I work for . . . , and the list goes on and on. I do not exist in a vacuum but in a tightly woven tapestry. And I've learned to love through its various threads and fabrics. And that's why a book given to me years ago seemed heaven sent. It's called *The Five Love Languages*. And it was another grace-filled light showing me the way through life's foggy paths.

The Five Love Languages

Years ago, a coworker noticed that I was having problems navigating love relationships and was kind enough to give me a copy of *The Five Love*

Languages by Gary Chapman. I see it now as another time God's grace was working through a believing Christian who had also been brought through a storm by that same grace. She and I would have long conversations in the mornings in the greenroom about loves lost and heartache. When she handed me the book, it was out of joy. I have since given the book to several family members and friends. One famous musician was so grateful for it that he told me it should be standard reading material for every person alive. It explains so much about who we are and why we do the things we do.

Years after reading the book, I was privileged to not only meet Dr. Gary Chapman, but interview him as well. He's a relationship counselor and a person of faith, so mild mannered and genteel. Dr. Chapman explained in his book how people can be passionately in love and have such hopes and dreams for their life together, but they are ignorant that they're two faulted, imperfect, and sinful people. And their arguments, squabbles, and conflicts are directly linked to the fact that they are speaking different love languages.

The five basic love languages are acts of service, personal touch, gift giving, words of affirmation, and quality time. Each of these love languages is filled with the grammar, parts of speech, and punctuation that any language has. It has dialects, nonverbal forms, and jargons that native speakers understand. Our first language, our native tongue, is the most powerful language we have. It is how we translate every other love language and understand a second, third, and fourth language, if we're so lucky to be able to learn another language. Our first language is our foundation and is used to construct every other tongue. We learn language basic to our beings.

You'll have to read the book for more details and examples, but my huge takeaway from the book and from talking with Dr. Chapman is that we all speak a primary love language. And we not only give love in that language, but it's how we need to receive it. And if we don't receive it in that language, we don't feel bathed and surrounded by love.

But, and it's a huge interjection: God speaks all love languages. Whatever kind of love we've learned to speak, it's only a pocket translator through which God can carry on a conversation with us. And this became a source of powerful hope for me, to find God in my life, holding on to me, picking me up when I am down, and loving me. When I need words of affirmation, what better source is there than God's Word? "You are the light of the world" (Matt. 5:14). When I need quality time, I go to God in prayer and "pray without ceasing" (1 Thess. 5:17 NKJV). When I feel that I deserve some act of service, I know it is God telling me to find a way to serve others, to build the church. "Rendering service with a good will as to the Lord and not to man" (Eph. 6:7 ESV). And when I require a loving physical touch, there's no other form than to ask for a hug and to be reminded of God: "You have enclosed me behind and before, and laid Your hand upon me" (Ps. 139:5 NASB). And when I seek to receive gifts for Christmas or birthdays, I am reminded that the best gift in all of history is Jesus Christ: "For God so loved the world that he gave his one and only Son, that whoever believes in him shall not perish but have eternal life" (John 3:16).

God's love through Jesus Christ is love in its most pure form. And this brings me to "The greatest of these . . ." (1 Cor. 13:13).

THE GREATEST OF THESE

I first learned the love verses in First Corinthians from the King James Version of the Bible. In that translation the word for *love* is "charity." "The greatest of these is charity." In his book *The Four Loves*, C. S. Lewis described variations of love we all experience: affection, friendship, eros, and charity. All love is not the same. There are different kinds and each has parameters. The affection a parent has for a child or between siblings is not the same as the brotherly love for a fellow citizen or the romantic feelings for a spouse. But charity stands as the greatest of these, as the godlike love we can only imitate. It's full of mercy, compassion, and sacrifice. And the only way Lewis can revel in this kind of love is to, as I have done, return to the garden. He said, "When God planted a garden He set a man over it and set the man under Himself. When He planted the garden of our nature and caused the flowering, fruiting loves to grow there, he set our will to 'dress' them. Compared with them it is dry and cold. And unless His grace comes down, like the rain and the sunshine, we shall use this tool to little purpose."[7]

We live in God's garden, or his vineyard, where he has created the soil, planted the seeds, and provided for loves, proper growth, and harmonious habitat. No love can be more pure than when God is our guiding light. And no love can face more potential defects than when something other than God becomes our ultimate trust. Lewis was saying that our wills have watered where they should not, and our loves have not grown according to plan. Now each of us is trying to find his or her way back to the garden, hacking away at the weeds we ourselves have let flourish.

The story of the garden is the grand narrative of humanity. And I can't help but recall something quite profound a psychologist told me about our own life stories. And how this garden is the solution to all our problems.

People Are Stories

A few years ago, I happened to have a conversation with Dr. Keith Ablow, a psychologist who's also a television commentator. It's one of the advantages of working at a television network. Experts from every field are all around in the hallways and in the offices. Casual talks can yield information. Dr. Ablow brings insight into news stories that go beyond the who, what, and where. His expertise helps explain the why behind some of the most gripping news like mass shootings and heinous murders. He also has a way of helping to explain the human condition. So I asked him once, "Do you see any big-picture description of who we are as people? Is there something that sort of sums up life?"

And he said, "Yes." And his answer was so simple and yet incredibly profound. He continued, "People are stories."

"Stories?" I repeated. I got his meaning but was perplexed at how this man of scientific training summed up the human experience using a literary device.

Not only are people stories, he said, but "the early stages and early chapters of our life stories . . . can determine the way we behave for decades."

But there was something else more fascinating. Not only are each of us a story, but there is a backstory to our lives which, and here I'm going to switch metaphors, provides the soil in which we were planted. The backstory of our earthly lives is the story of our parents before us, and their parents, and their parents before them. Those stories provide the soil of our *terroir*.

Here's how Dr. Ablow explained it. He said, "If you asked people to open a book, a novel, and asked them to start reading on page 179, then read to page 279, and then ask them to write the ending, people would say, 'I don't know these characters, I want to read the first 179 pages.'

"Well, in our lives, most of us never get to read the 179 pages. We're trying to write the finishing chapters while the first eleven chapters are glued together and we haven't even glanced at them. We are strangers to our own backstories."

In other words, we are strangers to the kind of soil in which we are growing.

Dr. Ablow gave me an example. He said, "Let's say a woman had obtrusive parents, no control in her life. She's hurt by that and traumatized. . . . But, such a woman might be on a program, a software program that says, 'Never let someone close to you that's powerful, because that person will overwhelm you and you'll lose your personhood.' So she might marry three men in a row who are weak. And when they fall apart and become alcoholics or can't earn a living, [she] might be mystified, 'Why is this happening to me?'"

Dr. Ablow said that woman may be thinking to herself, "'I'm not lovable. The world isn't fair. Men always fall apart.' When what she should be saying is, 'If I were to allow myself to be more vulnerable, even though I was hurt the first time by people so close to me, I could be loved and things could go really well for me.'"

Dr. Ablow's story of this woman reminded me of a conversation I overheard on a flight. The woman behind me was a professional organizer. She was explaining to the person seated next to her that her upbringing was quite dysfunctional. She didn't go into much detail, but said that becoming uber-organized was a way to have some sort of control in her life. In that situation, her backstory helped her achieve a modicum of success.

But there are many backstories that produce tragic endings. And this is where Dr. Ablow's analysis should make us all shudder with fear.

A murder that captivated the nation was the case of Scott Peterson. Peterson was convicted of killing his eight-months-pregnant wife Laci and dumping her body in the San Francisco Bay. The case was so perplexing because the Petersons appeared to be the perfect young couple, happy and excited about the birth of their first child. But underneath Scott's cool and personable exterior, said Dr. Ablow, who wrote about the case, was a tumultuous undercurrent created by an even more dysfunctional heritage.

"Very often the roots of violence today, or pathology today," said Dr. Ablow, "reaches back easily three or four or five generations. And you can see catastrophe coming like a freight train down the tracks."

Scott Peterson's mother had been raised in an orphanage, separated from her brother who was also placed in an orphanage.

"The orphanage separated her from her brother so she also lost all contact with her brother. When she emerged from the orphanage, hoping to take care of her mother who was ill, . . . her mother then died precipitously. So this hope of a [unified family] . . . bust again.

"What did she do? She tried to create families. So she got pregnant twice by two different men hoping to get a family. Each time she got pregnant they left her. And what did she do? She put these kids up for adoption right away. The third time it happened, the powers that be, the social service people said, 'You can't keep giving kids up for adoption. You have to keep this kid.' Well, that kid was Scott Peterson. And the man she ended up marrying to raise Scott Peterson had left his marriage, because why? He didn't like kids.

"So you have Scott Peterson raised by a woman who herself was given away, who gave away two other kids, who's married to a man who gave away kids. Scott Peterson, having been raised in an atmosphere where they couldn't stand him, is now pregnant [with wife Laci] and is about to join a family. And there's no way that's going to happen.

"So the idea that his wife is pregnant, and that's the moment at which he decides, 'No, it's better if she and the baby drown' [it's not certain how they were killed] is foretold at least two generations, and no doubt more."

If what Dr. Ablow said is true, then within our own stories we all carry the seeds of our own demise; the seeds of the weeds that will take over our vineyards. Each one of us is a complicated mishmash of experiences. We are vines growing in a vineyard we didn't plant, and yet we are bound to grow whether we choose to or not.

The Garden's Grand Narrative

But what Dr. Ablow forgot is that there is another backstory that overrides our own. And instead of attaching ourselves to the story of our faulted families, we have a grand narrative to which we can bind ourselves to; it is the story of God's love for his creation. A love that never fails, a love that transcends and transforms any life challenges, because it is a love that says, "I give my life so that you may live, so that you may get back to my garden, my vineyard." It's true that to grow in the proper way, the way God intended, we have to get back to the root of the problem as Dr. Ablow suggested. To put it another way, we have to understand the law of the root, as my friend Dr. Ravi Zacharias says. It means that a plant's strength depends on how the seed is nurtured and how it is cared for, with its roots reaching deep into the divine water table. And the only perfect seed that grew into a perfect vine is Jesus. He is the vine. And we are only branches. We must be grafted onto that perfect vine. And when that happens, his roots become our roots. No matter what life has thrown at you, no matter what your DNA has brought you, God's law of the root is a pathway to his love.

Morning in the Vineyard

It is now morning again in the vineyard. I am at once imagining a morning several centuries ago in another garden, when a woman encountered a most extraordinary man. He greeted her outside the tomb of her beloved teacher who had been most brutally killed three days before. She met who she believed was the gardener. Who she met was the Gardener. She met a person. She met Love himself. She met the risen Savior, Jesus. He is the great Gardener, his sacrifice on the cross the climax of humanity's grand narrative.

The complexity of who we are and who we were meant to be is best understood through our loves. And how we learn to love comes from the world around us. And the processes of learning to love, getting love, and holding on to love make us the protagonist in our own stories. But how different will our stories end if we see not ourselves but Jesus as protagonist, as the leading figure directing and moving our stories?

How then can we be transformed by that story? So far on our journey we've explored the strength of the *covenant* and the love found in the *sacrifice*; now we need to encounter him in one more place. It is time to venture into one more divine realm: the place of the Holy Spirit, the place of worship. We must see Jesus in the *glory*.

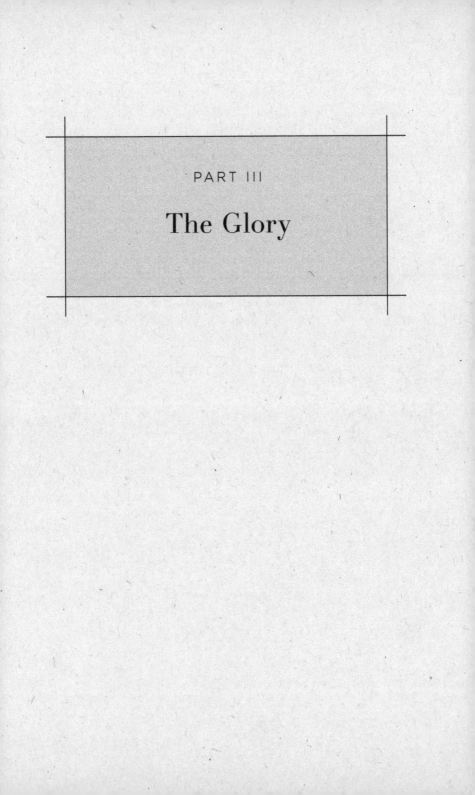

PART III

The Glory

CHAPTER 8

The Song of My Soul

Who is he, this King of glory? The LORD
Almighty—he is the King of glory.

—PSALM 24:10

I WILL NEVER FULLY LEAVE BEHIND THE LESSONS learned in the vineyard. God's abounding love is now a forceful presence, providing a keener insight into some of the most perplexing parts of my job as a journalist. Why do people do bad things? These are the stories that make the news. And these are the stories that make me.

Of the five w's of basic journalism—who, what, when, where, and why—the why is the most compelling. It often keeps stories in the headlines and the public eye. It's especially the case with murders, particularly one I remember involving a husband, wife, and their unborn child. They were in their car leaving a birthing class near Boston in 1989. The wife, seven months pregnant, was shot and killed by an "unknown, black assailant." The husband was wounded in the attack, shot in the leg. He drove wounded, trying to find help on the phone with police as they desperately tried to locate him. The community's collective outrage and horror knew no bounds. But as police investigated further, they realized that there had been no anonymous criminal responsible, that the unknown assailant was the husband who shot his wife for the insurance money and shot himself to make it look like they were both victims.[1]

The story still haunts me today. Why would someone do such a thing? But as I began to understand who we are and who God is, and what his love means as a reality for our daily lives, stories like these and others started to make more sense, although the answer is even scarier than I imagined, because it means all of us are susceptible, are capable of equally as heinous a crime.

Please don't be offended. For those of us who never faced the awful truth of our own sinful nature, this can be quite a shock. But hear me out, because there's incredible hope for us all as well. And that hope has a simple prescription on the one hand, but on the other may be a hard pill to swallow. All of our misdeeds and misguided choices stem from something we all do every day of our lives, and that is worship. You may not believe this idea, and I can understand why. It took me a while to believe this as a reality too. We're all so sure we're independent agents making our own decisions, following our hearts desires, doing what we believe is the right thing. And when someone who's raised in the "right way" with all the trappings of a good upbringing goes off the rails and does something so out of character, we're perplexed. But in fact, the whole of our lives are controlled by what one minister calls "deep idols,"[2] that third rail that powers and defines who we are. And that can be anything, wealth and prosperity, good looks, political power. And we'll sacrifice just about anything to have it, if the conditions are right.

That man who shot his wife had been worshipping wealth and status. He had made a covenant with the idol of success, whatever that was in his mind. He'd bowed down to it, was a slave to it. And when he had failed to do his Master's will, he sacrificed his wife and unborn child to his idol in the hopes of appeasing its demands.

This is now how I look at all news stories. I say to myself, "What idol, what false god is this person bowing to that made them do what they did?" Here's a short list of some headlines:

"Husband Arrested After Pediatrician Wife Stabbed to Death in
Shower," [3]
"Blood, Sweatpants and Tears: Man Bashed into Coma in Fight Vs.
Bro,"[4]
"Man Slashes Father Before Leaping to His Death from 46th Floor
Upper East Side Apartment,"[5] and
"Young Monsters: Girls, 12, 'Stabbed' Pal over Web Tale."[6]

These are all stories involving people with no prior criminal record. Just
everyday folk unaware of the false gods and idols they were worshipping.

RETURN TO THE LIGHTHOUSE

I began this book with the imagery of the lighthouse as a divine messenger,
a visual of God's Ten Commandments, emphasizing that the Decalogue
is not just a list of dos and don'ts of how we are to behave, but is rather a
template for all law, physical, spiritual, as well as moral. I explained that
the first commandment, which states, "I am the LORD your God. . . . You
shall have no other gods before me" (Ex. 20:2–3) is the light of the law,
defining its reason for being. It's just like the lamp of the lighthouse defines
its purpose for being. What this means about us is that if we are made in
the image of God, and this law describes his universal order in the world,
then we, too, must be defined by something. And what defines us gives us
our purpose in life. And as one minister says, what defines us is really our
Master. We don't control it. It controls us. We must bow down to what we
believe gives us our reason for being. Of course, now you see that God's
desire is for us to choose him as our master. Because only God can give us
what our hearts truly desire. But, and this is a big *but*, only a loving God
would give us the choice of whether or not to love him. And if we don't
consciously put him and his laws in the forefront of our daily living, then
we are all a potential headline waiting to be written.

If that's the case, then how do we get that power? How are we guided toward this act of worship that is apparently so important to the way our souls and bodies are meant to work? The answer is found in the Holy Spirit, the third member of the Trinity, the breath that carries the very Spirit of God and directs our worship.

THE HOLY SPIRIT

After his resurrection, Jesus came to the disciples in a locked room. He ate with them, talked with them, and preached to them. He then breathed on them and said, "Receive the Holy Spirit" (John 20:22). The Holy Spirit, the third member of the triune God, would be their catalyst, their sustainer in keeping the faith. God knew from his work with the Israelites, his chosen people, that even with his laws spoon-fed to them, they would find other gods to worship, ones that would not give them life but would drain it from them.

The Holy Spirit was always and is always our resource to worshipping the true God, and to avoid the worshipping of any false gods.

It is difficult to know where to begin exploring something as transcendent as the Holy Spirit. This ubiquitous Being has been present since the beginning of time as well, yet was only recognized as part of the godhead by the church fathers at the Council of Nicaea in the fourth century to combat the Arian controversy. Boy, were they ever busy. It would be so easy to dismiss the Holy Spirit's divinity for that reason alone. And many have.

But before you brush off the Holy Spirit as inconsequential, consider this: think about the pervasiveness of electricity. It powers ours homes, office buildings, whole cities, and all our modern conveniences. It is a physical phenomenon but has no physical body. We can see it sometimes in its most scary and dramatic displays as lightning, causing fires and widespread destruction. But there are also milder forms, like electric currents producing static electricity that makes hair stand on end and gives a shock when a door handle is touched. The most important thing to remember here is that scientists and inventors (like Ben Franklin, whose famous experiment with the kite on a string with a key brought lightning out of the clouds and into our homes; and Thomas Edison, who brought us the lightbulb) didn't invent electricity. They discovered it. Electricity had been in the world since the beginning of time as electromagnetism, one of the four forces of physics. All man did was discover how to order it, harnessing its power and its benefits for the flourishing of humanity.

I would like to think of the Holy Spirit in somewhat the same way but on a far grander scale. He has been operating since before "in the beginning . . ." (Gen. 1:1). I don't think it's possible to control the Holy Spirit, but I do think it's possible to understand his divine and glorious power. If we recognize the Spirit's power and submit to his authority to lead us to the Almighty.

THE LIGHT OF YOUR SPIRIT

To understand more of the Holy Spirit's power, let us return again to the lighthouse, standing strong and tall on the edge of a precipice or in the midst of troubling seas. See the light in the lighthouse? It's the lamp burning inside, pointing the way to safety. And remember that the light defines the lighthouse's whole purpose for being.

Now, imagine yourself to *be* a lighthouse, planted firmly in a world that you did not create, but a world that has created you. Ask yourself, "On what or to whom is my light pointing? To what do I look to for safety? On what or whom does my light shine?" We cannot look to ourselves because we are part of the mechanism.

The light of the lighthouse looks out; it does not look inward. It looks out to find, to search for lost souls. However, our light searches not to find, but to be found. This is the dilemma of the human heart. It looks for that which will give it purpose and a reason for being. This is glory. This is the act of worship. It is holding something up and bowing down to it. Of shining your light *on* something, *around* it, and *through* it, believing it will define the purpose of your light.

The Holy Spirit is the one that directs our light to God. Its job is to lead us to the One who can keep our lights burning bright, powering them and giving them their true purpose.

Whether we worship the God of the Bible or the flying spaghetti monster, it's all part of our existential DNA. All of us worship, even the most ardent atheist. How do I know?

Why do atheists like Richard Dawkins and Sam Harris write books, lecture, or debate Christians? It's because they are evangelists for their faith in no divine being. They are invested in their belief that there is no God. But it is a belief all the same, because while there's no empirical proof that God exists, there's no proof he does not. So all of us make a leap of faith. You may not go to church every Sunday or pray, but all of us hold up something or a lot of things as worthy of our praise, our allegiance, our trust, and our joy. If you're not worshipping God, you're worshipping something else. This is the act of glorification. This is the glory, to bow to that which defines you. And we modern-day people with all our technology and advanced knowledge are following the pattern of tens of thousands of generations before us.

THE BEGINNINGS OF WORSHIP

Here may be some proof that we all worship something. Let's travel back to Turkey eleven thousand years ago to an ancient archeological site called Göbekli Tepe. Archeologists first discovered it in 1960 but thought it nothing more than an ancient cemetery. All their education and knowledge told them that religion sprang up after human beings began cultivating agriculture, growing food where they settled instead of living in small nomadic bands foraging food as best they could.

But in the early 1990s, a German archeologist named Klaus Schmidt discovered something that all the previous scientists had missed. The "massive stone pillars arranged into a set of rings, one mashed up against the next" was not a burial site.[7] It was a temple, the first of its kind. And it predates Stonehenge by about six thousand years. The find turned conventional wisdom on its head. It showed that instead of man creating religion because they now had the time after building stable communities, humanity's need to worship came first.

"We used to think agriculture gave rise to cities and later writing, art, and religion. Now the world's oldest temple suggests the urge to worship sparked civilization."[8]

It doesn't matter what they worshipped eleven thousand years ago in Göbekli Tepe. The site confirms what God's law has stated all along: that we need to worship, to have something in which to put our ultimate trust, as if worshipping is as important as our need to breathe. Worship doesn't just give meaning to our lives. Worship is life. And none of us can avoid it.

There isn't a culture on the globe that does not worship. C. S. Lewis in his landmark writing *Mere Christianity* said it shouldn't be surprising that in all cultures there's not only worship, but that many of the moral codes are quite similar.

> If anyone will take the trouble to compare the moral teaching of, say, the ancient Egyptians, Babylonians, Hindus, Chinese, Greeks and Romans, what will really strike him will be how very like they are to each other and to our own. Men have differed as regards what people you ought to be unselfish to—whether it was only your own family, or your fellow countrymen, or every one. But they have always agreed that you ought not to put yourself first. Selfishness has never been admired. Men have differed as to whether you should have one wife or four. But they have always agreed that you must not simply have any woman you liked.[9]

To his point, C. S. Lewis makes the case that it would be surprising if we *didn't* have all these similar rules and ancient stories. If the Bible is true, that all are made in the image of God, not just those who've been shaped by the Judeo-Christian doctrine, then we should find something universal about us, binding us together as one, as actors in a world that is, as Calvin phrased, "a theatre of the glory of God."[10]

In the previous two sections of this book, the Covenant and the Sacrifice, there were physical correlations that we could look to. In covenant, the unwavering laws give us architecture, physical buildings. In sacrifice, the decay and death bring us agriculture, gardens, vineyards, and how life grows. But what about glory, what is the earthly equivalent of something as ethereal and transcendent as the Holy Spirit?

I can tell you from my own experience as a pianist that there is nothing more powerful and more a depiction of an invisible force of glory than music.

THE SOURCE OF LOVE: GLORY

Most of us could tell a story about a certain piece of music that evokes incredible emotion, joy or sorrow; some song or symphony that takes you to a different place and time. A friend of mine told me that he can't listen to "Amazing Grace" without weeping because it was the hymn played at his father's funeral.

I always think of my great-aunt Wreatha whenever "Beautiful Savior" is sung in church. It was one of her favorite hymns.

Every year at Christmas time I give a caroling party. I invite everyone I know: friends, family, work colleagues. It's gotten quite a reputation these last few years of being one of the best holiday parties in New York City. Somehow we manage to crowd about sixty or more people into my apartment, which is large by Manhattan standards, but not large enough to accommodate that many people without challenging everyone's personal space. But I'm always surprised how much people love the singing of carols. There's a pleasure in singing that gets to the core of human expression.

I've sung those Christmas carols for decades. But a few years ago was the first time the carols spoke to me in a way that they never had before. The words of the carols I had sung since childhood became real to me. I understood them not as a child who likes the melodies or because it means toys are on the way, but as an adult, a mature Christian who finally understood the meaning of Jesus' birth, of God becoming man, and his sacrifice on the cross. The words of "Hark! The Herald Angels Sing" and "Joy to the

World" brought tears to my eyes. The words leapt off the printed page and into my heart as if I were singing them for the first time: "Veiled in flesh the Godhead see; hail the incarnate Deity, pleased as man with us to dwell, Jesus our Emmanuel, Hark the herald angels sing, Glory to the new born king!"[11]

Or, "Joy to the world! the Lord is come: let earth receive her King. Let every heart prepare him room, and heaven and nature sing!"[12]

There's so much depth of theology and doctrine in those words: "Veiled in flesh the Godhead see." This is "the Word became flesh" (1:14) that the gospel writer John spoke of: the godhead of the Father, Son, and Holy Spirit. It is now veiled, covered in flesh, appearing by outward standards as just another human being. But he is welcomed, "hailed" as king, an earthly deity. Or the second verse of "Joy to the World": "He rules the world with truth and grace. . . . Far as the curse is found."[13] This moved me to tears. His blessings will flow to all of us because we are all subject to the curse of Adam's fall from grace. And he rules! Not with an iron sword, but with truth, which directs the mind, and grace, which melts the heart. He rules with those twin scepters.

But the tears welling up in my eyes were not a reaction to doctrine. It was a response to the gospel, to finally understanding the depth of love that God had for me. It was beyond mere words. It took music to put it into my soul.

How is it that the hearing and singing of these words together make such a powerful emotional impact? To see the words in print and to read them have nearly no impact at all. They are words on a piece of paper taken in as information. But in their musical form suddenly they have a meaning that they had not had before. It is the same with many of the great hymns of the church, "Be Still My Soul," "Pass Me Not O Gentle Savior," and of course, "How Great thou Art."

I am not alone in music's effect.

THE POWER OF MUSIC

Music is ubiquitous in this world. Every culture has it and uses it in much the same way. Music has the ability to mold cultures, create them, and sustain them. At the Olympics the athlete who takes the gold medal will hear his or her country's national anthem. In America at the beginning of sports events our anthem is played as well. Universities and colleges have school songs. "The Star-Spangled Banner" reminds us of the Fourth of July and fireworks. "The Battle Hymn of the Republic" is an ode to the burdens of the Civil War.

In music we can see glory's effects. It is something ethereal that is at once awesome and inspirational, as well as potent and sometimes dangerous. It is a quality that both leads us and pushes us, taking us to places we didn't know we wanted to go, but once there realize it's where we belong. This, too, describes the power of the Holy Spirit, the third member of the Trinity, the godhead of Father, Son, and Holy Ghost, as he "fulfills an ongoing but invisible role of connection and communication between people and God."[14]

From before the beginning of creation this entity of spirit has been present "hovering over the waters" (Gen. 1:2), the force behind bringing chaos into order, breathing life into Adam (2:7), leading the Israelites out of Egypt with a pillar of fire by night and pillar of smoke by day (Ex. 13:21). It is the Paraclete who "comes alongside the believer to 'guide into all truth.'"[15] It is the image of a dove upon the shoulder of Jesus following his baptism in the Jordan River, and the voice of God saying, "This is my Son . . . with him I am well pleased" (Matt. 3:17). While God is the speaker, Jesus is the speech, and the Holy Spirit is the breath that carries it.[16]

Only music can mimic such a lofty plane. The air transports it to our bodies, into our auditory systems, vibrating in our bones and sinew as it's carried along the pulsating rhythms of our own heartbeats, which pump the blood to every part of our bodies. The blood. Again it's the blood. It reaches to even there, to what gives us life. Nothing else on earth is like music. Nor can anything on earth grasp its power. Music to me is God's way of showing us that there is a deeper part of who we are, that there is a depth in our souls that the outside everyday world cannot reach.

Music shows us and helps us experience a level of life that we could not otherwise experience. It penetrates our psyches, making a beeline straight to the real people we are and what we are made for. We are made to worship. We are made to bow down and submit to something greater than ourselves. Good music pleases us. "Great music evangelizes."[17] It is designed to give glory, to lift mankind's soul from the here and now, to give a glimpse of eternity, transporting it to the heavens, soaring to heights where only the angels can see. This is music; one's body can hardly contain the spirit, which wants to burst from its earthly flesh and be one with the music.

But why does music have such power over us? Do we choose to let it have power? No, it chooses us. As we explored earlier in chapter 7 regarding language acquisition and love, it is involuntary and our souls acquiesce. Can you honestly say you can listen to the beat of the "Stars and Stripes Forever" and not be affected, inwardly marching with it? How about a waltz? Doesn't your body sway without effort to the three-quarter beat? If you're in a restaurant and the waiters suddenly start singing "Happy Birthday" to a patron, can you really keep silent? Even if you don't sing along, all conversations stop to listen to the music.

Then there's the power of music in movies. Music tells us how to feel at any moment in the story, happy, sad, bold, or triumphant. In fact, music is the story. Can anyone hear the thumping, ominous low notes of the theme from *Jaws* without feeling even a hint of trepidation? That two-note theme tells you the monster of the deep blue is near and about to devour his prey.

To show how much music makes a film, consider the effect when it's not there. In one of the greatest horror flicks ever made, there is no music. Alfred Hitchcock's *The Birds* has no musical soundtrack. The only sounds we hear accompanying the story are the flapping of the bird's wings, their screeching and violent chirping. Deep down, we long to hear music, to console and to warn, and yet there is none. It makes the film that much scarier. On some deeper level we are forced to feel that the birds are truly in charge. And although we long to hear some soothing, audible landscape, there is none to hold on to. Even though that movie was made more than fifty years ago with nowhere near the special effects of today's computer-generated realism, it still has the effect of scaring us half to death. And it's because Hitchcock understood that without music, the audience would have nowhere to turn for safety.

PROFESSOR OF MUSIC

One person who has had a great influence over my understanding of music and faith is Dr. Jeremy Begbie, a professor of music and theology at Duke University in North Carolina, and also at Cambridge University in England. He's got so much energy it seems he could light up a midsized house just by walking in front of it. He's an incredible concert pianist and a theological scholar who has combined the power of music with the knowledge of Scripture. He's the one who first told me about the lack of musical sounds in the movie *The Birds*. I talked with him about this idea of the three-part design—of covenant, sacrifice, and glory—and particularly the power music has over us and yet how unaware we are of it.

I asked, "Are we blind to music's effects?"

Jeremy answered, "Even in the church sometimes, people will . . . very often times tend to think of [it as] a frill. 'Why do you bother with something so frivolous in life? It doesn't actually do anything.' And yet," he said, "they spend hundreds of dollars a year, thousands of dollars a year on music, iphone or ipod, music-playing apparatus. It's very interesting. In our culture one part of us says it's not important, but our behavior tells a different story. Why is it?"

I pointed out that the power of music has not escaped the powers that be. Napoleon is said to have stated, "Show me who controls the music of a society, and I care not who makes its laws."

Dr. Begbie was quick to concur. "Of course totalitarian regimes [understood]. That's why they censored it so carefully. The Taliban banned music, as you know. Hundreds of historical figures have seen that music really does make a difference. And wise people who run worship services realize it, too, that you can make or break a service with music."

Dr. Begbie lectured about music and its power, giving insight into something that we hear and are affected by daily. Music is an art form, but it's one we cannot see. We listen to it, but we can't put a score of Beethoven's Ninth Symphony, the famous "Ode to Joy," in a frame and revel at its dulcet tones and driving rhythms. We must hear its tones wafting through the air.

It is why music is like God in that way, and certainly the Holy Spirit. We cannot simply have God as information, as notes on a page. God must be experienced.

"Exactly!" said Dr. Begbie. "He's not a digit. He can't be packaged as a bit of information. No, God makes himself known by taking us into a narrative."[18]

The Bible and Music

I've played piano all my life and studied it at the University of Minnesota. I've performed recitals and concerts and accompanied other musicians for fun and for pay. But it wasn't until the last decade or so that I fully absorbed how much the Scriptures have to say about music.

The Bible is rife with musical references. Making music to God is one of the most stated directives in the holy Scriptures. In the Old Testament, every aspect of the Israelites' lives was marked by it: worship, war, peace, rituals. The longest book in the entire Bible is a songbook, the book of Psalms. And in the book of Psalms, followers are commanded some two hundred times to make music to God.

"Sing to the LORD a new song; sing to the LORD, all the earth." (Ps. 96:1)

"Begin the music, strike the timbrel, play the melodious harp and lyre." (81:2)

"Worship the LORD with gladness; come before him with joyful songs." (100:2)

But music was also used to corrupt. In the book of Daniel, Babylon's King Nebuchadnezzar used music to demand fealty of his subjects, that at the sound of the instruments everyone should bow down before him: "Therefore, as soon as they heard the sound of the horn, flute, zither, lyre, harp and all kinds of music, all the nations and people of every language fell down and worshiped the image of gold that King Nebuchadnezzar had set up" (Dan. 3:7).

No musical instrument in the Bible has more power and pathos than the trumpet. In the Old Testament, at its sound, the Israelites shouted and the walls of Jericho came tumbling down (Josh. 6:5).

For Gideon and his band of three hundred warriors, the blowing of the trumpet was a rallying cry as they went to battle against the Midianites. Even the horse knew the sound of the trumpet was a call to war and knew what was required of it: "In frenzied excitement it eats up the ground; it cannot stand still when the trumpet sounds" (Job 39:24).

In the New Testament in Paul's letter to the Corinthians, he told them of how the trumpet would signal those being resurrected in Christ: "For the trumpet will sound, the dead will be raised imperishable, and we will be changed" (1 Cor. 15:52).

And it is the trumpet that will sound at the end of time when God will assign Satan to the lake of fire and all will be as it should have been back in Eden before the fall: "The seventh angel sounded his trumpet, and there were loud voices in heaven, which said: 'The kingdom of the world has become the kingdom of our Lord and of his Messiah, and he will reign for ever and ever'" (Rev. 11:15). Hallelujah!

The sound of the trumpet is the sound of victory, God's victory.

From a biblical point of view music is a powerful force, there's no doubt. But from a scientific point of view music is a powerful mystery. That it affects us is certain. But *why* it affects us is a scientific uncertainty. This whole book has been getting to the root causes for what makes this whole universe work and our lives within it. What of God's law and love can we find in the study of music that might give clues to this amazing mystery of covenant, sacrifice, and glory? Is there a divine message hidden within music's physical nature that gives us a clue as to why it has intrinsic power? And more important, why, just like the Holy Spirit, does it have such power over us?

CHAPTER 9

The Song of My Heart

As a musician, I have always been warmed by William Shakespeare's opening words in his play *Twelfth Night*, that, "If music be the food of love, play on."[1] The sentiment seems the most appropriate explanation of music's calling as the sustenance of true love. It's taken almost my entire lifetime of studying music to arrive at the point where I would now argue that this craft has an even higher calling: to satisfy the soul, to soothe the longing in the heart, and to quench the mind's thirst for transcendent truths.

It is the Holy Spirit who has brought me on such a quest. So Holy Spirit, lead on.

We know music is powerful. But not all music is pleasant. Why are some musical sounds pleasing to us? Why are others not? In other words, why are some musical sounds discordant, disturbing, or, to use the musical technical word, *dissonant*? When a toddler bangs on a piano keyboard combining every note her fingers and elbows can reach, her parents may tell her to stop making that racket! When a five-year-old begins to learn violin, the screeches and scratches are enough to make our spines ache. But how about if that same child were playing a Bach's prelude or a hymn, or even a popular song, getting all the notes right, of course, and playing in tune? Why is that ordered sound more enjoyable to listen to?

Does this point to what we could call a "substantive universal"[2] in music, as the great composer and conductor Leonard Bernstein claimed, which unites us all in a common experience? Does that universal foundation also create metaphysical connections between mankind and a creator? Is there any proof of that connection between music and an omniscient, omnipotent Being? And if so, how exactly does music fully embody the third element in our study of God's law and love, the glory?

As I said in the previous chapter, God has commanded us some two hundred times in the book of Psalms alone to make music to him. If music didn't have a divine calling, why would God bother giving us this directive about something that some schools consider extracurricular?

What is this "food of love" made of?

Recent research on music and the brain shows that music is biologically a deeply ingrained function of the human brain. Michael Thaut wrote, "The brain has neural circuitry that is dedicated to music. Music is associated with a specific yet complex brain architecture."[3]

A plethora of research has come out in the last two decades about the ability of early music training in children to develop spatial reasoning skills, suggesting "that music training generates the neural connections used for abstract reasoning, including those necessary for understanding mathematical concepts."[4] A Canadian study showed that weekly training in piano or voice increased children's IQs by nearly three points more than their "untrained peers."[5]

Here's a really good example. Albert Einstein, one of the greatest geniuses of all time, "reveled in mathematics and music. . . . By the age of twelve Einstein became deeply religious, combining ardent belief in God with a passion for the music of Mozart and Beethoven, and composed songs to the glory of God which he sang aloud to himself on his way to and back from school."[6]

In Gordon Shaw's book most known for introducing us to the "Mozart effect," he said that "music and mathematics are causally linked through the built-in, innate ability of the brain to recognize symmetries and use them to see how patterns develop in space and time."[7]

Theoretical physicist Dr. Michio Kaku concurred, succinctly saying, "The human brain is a pattern seeking machine."[8] And music with its regulated frequencies, rhythmic melodies, and harmonic progressions is a magnet for brains like ours.

As neurologist Dr. Oliver Sacks pointed out, it's one of the reasons Madison Avenue invests so heavily in commercial jingles. Patterns of short, catchy tunes can form *brain worms* that tunnel deep in our gray matter, embedding in our psyches and becoming tunes that we can't get out of our heads. We don't even have to recall the actual tune for the jingle to jiggle our minds into buying a product, or at least look favorably toward it.

Let's look at it first from a purely physiological standpoint. When we hear music, it registers initially in the limbic system of our brains, the area primarily concerned with emotion. The music is then beamed to the frontal cortex, the youngest part of our brains, the seat of language and reasoning and problem solving. The frontal cortex is fed and nurtured by the complexities music presents, affecting the structure of the developing brain. Remember Dr. Tukey and his research on synaptic development. Music helps form those neurological pathways.

The physiological responses to music are impressive as well. Music has a significant effect on pulse and respiration and has been shown to lower blood pressure. Studies on stroke victims found that rhythm could help improve the injured brain. Music also inhibits muscular fatigue. For instance, if you're exercising, playing music will help you work out longer and run farther.

Dr. Sacks recalled a young autistic boy who could not learn to tie his shoe even after repeated attempts. When music was added to the learning process, he accomplished the task on the second try.

But music also has its ill effects. There are people who suffer a rare condition where epileptic seizures are triggered by music. And certain types of rock and acid rock music can do physical harm to your brain. Dr. Leslie A. Chambers showed that proteins in a liquid medium were coagulated when subjected to piercing high-pitched sounds. Laurence O'Donnell cited in an article on music and the brain how a former rock musician remembered "in the 70's, teens would bring raw eggs to a rock concert and put them on the front of the stage. The eggs would be hard boiled by the music before the end of the concert and could be eaten."[9]

This is the effect some rock music has on your brain. When rock stars' brains are fried, they really could be hard-boiled!

THE SCIENCE ISN'T ENOUGH

But human beings are not just scientific biological units. They are both rational *and* relational beings, needing intellectual stimulation as well as compassion, love, and intimacy. God knows this too. The result is that the scientific facts about music can't fully satisfy.

Why are our emotions so swayed and controlled by mere strains of sustained sounds when they are harmoniously grouped? Why have many people, myself included, called music as close to the divine as a living soul can be? U-2 front man Bono said, "Words and music . . . introduced me to God, not belief in God, more an experiential sense of God."[10]

Is God in the music? Or does the music simply allow us an intense experience in any time or space we happen to be?

Music is the embodiment of science and faith that we've kept separated for far too long. The only way to fully understand music's power over us is to bring these two interrelated parts together.

And in so doing, we may discover that music is a connection to an abiding and unconditional love; a love that, "surpasses all understanding" (Phil. 4:7 ESV), a love that endures forever, a transcendent being. In other words, God.

The gospel writer John wrote, "God is love" (1 John 4:8). This reference states that love is more than one of God's attributes. It is the very essence of who he is. I take that to mean that God is love like water is wet. And if that is so, then all the laws of the physical universe like gravity, electromagnetism, and photosynthesis are products of God's love. That would also include the laws of what makes music, music. With that in mind, taking another look at Duke Orsino's words in *Twelfth Night*, we may call Shakespeare a theologian as well as a playwright. For the opening sentiments of his play may be a powerful insight into the nature of music and its ability to bring us in tune with the living God, that music is God's way of not only leading us to him, but letting him be our sole source of sustenance.

MUSIC'S DIVINE POWER

Let's suppose the laws governing music were more than physics. What if the laws of theory and harmony were divine rules? Music could then be considered the conduit between the mind and the soul, perhaps even a two-way transmitter for speaking to God and receiving God's message.

Bear with me as I present a basic minicourse in music theory, what all young musicians learn on some rudimentary level, and all music majors learn to a more advanced level. Music theory can seem daunting at first, like mathematic equations essentially, especially if you have no musical background. But I assure you the payoff will be incredible. Because I believe that understanding this physical reality of music will help explain its power: that hidden within the science of music is its divine message.

Let's begin.

THE SCIENCE OF MUSIC: PYTHAGORAS, STRING RATIOS, OVERTONES, AND MUSIC THEORY

We know from science that the nature of music is based in physics. It is vibratory in its nature. Each tone is made of hundreds and thousands of beats per second, or frequencies, that our ears hear as sustained sound. Low notes have fewer beats per second; high notes have more frequent beats per second. What's more, there's an order to the sound that man did not create. It is found in its physical nature, a discovery credited to sixth century BC Greek mathematician and philosopher Pythagoras, who figured largely in chapter 2 with his theorem on right-angle triangles. In the realm of music though, Pythagoras and his followers discovered music's mathematical formula that nature produced. It was a mathematical mystery waiting a few millennia to be unveiled, and a few hundred years more to be refined.[11]

The legend goes like this. One day Pythagoras, walking by a smithy shop, heard hammers clamoring. Occasionally the sounds of the hammers striking their targets simultaneously would be quite pleasing, sometimes they would be rather irritating, and he wondered why.

The hammers the smithys used were of different sizes. At first, Pythagoras thought it was the size of the man and his strength that made the difference, so he had them switch hammers. Low and behold the sounds were the same. It didn't matter how large the man was or his technique. What made the difference was the size of the hammer and specifically, the ratios between them. A ratio of one to two produced a sound twice as high.

He then transferred the science to strings of equal size, stretched at a certain tension. He discovered that when a string was halved, it sounded the same but higher; twice the frequency.

Pythagoras's next discovery was that if you played the strings at the same time, it produced a sound that was pleasing. What he found was that certain intervals (the distance between two notes) were pleasant to the ear, or *consonant*, and other sounds were not so pleasing, or *dissonant*. Chief among these pleasant intervals were the intervals of the *octave*, the *fourth*, and the *fifth*. Or explained in ratios: 2:1, the octave; 2:3, the fifth; 4:3, the fourth. Now the interval of the fifth is special. Keep that in mind as we proceed.

The Deep Magic

String ratios, however, are an indication of something deeper. There are facts supporting the idea that what makes certain sounds pleasing to our ears has to do with something transcendent that strings and other instruments produce, which is another example of what C. S. Lewis named the "deep magic."[12] This is the part of music that goes further into the mystical world of mathematics, prompting many people to believe that God himself is a mathematician. For it is the mathematical relationship between notes that brings us harmony. *Harmony* means how certain notes sound together. Some go well together, and others don't, causing tension that needs resolving. And what creates the formula for either is based on something called overtones.

WHAT IN THE WORLD ARE OVERTONES?

The mystery of why music has power over us begins to be solved when we look at a picture of a vibrating string. Captured today with high-speed cameras, the vibrating string looks almost ghostly, ethereal, even angelic. And when we see the vibrating string, we can see what is meant by overtones. Overtones are sounds a vibrating string produces that your ear *doesn't* hear that produces the sound your ear *does* hear. Let me repeat that because it's a critical point. Overtones are sounds you *don't hear* that produce the sounds you *do hear*. It may seem like science fiction, but I assure you it's a scientific fact. In John D. Barrow's captivating essay on mathematics, he pointed out that our ears are tuned to sound the way our eyes can perceive light.[13] In other words, our ears hear the sound version of the light of God. And overtones make it happen. Here's how.

When a string is plucked, or in the case of a piano when a key is played and a hammer hits a string, your ear hears one tone. But what's actually happening is you're hearing a series of tones. That's because the string is vibrating at the halfway point, at the quarter, the third, and on up the length of the string. That vibrating action on the string produces overtones. And each string has a fixed relationship with those overtones; the lower the overtone positioned on the string, the stronger the relationship to the sound you're hearing.

The sound the string makes when it's plucked is called the *fundamental tone*. The very existence of the overtones is generated by the fundamental tone. Now again, the relationship each overtone has with the fundamental tone depends on how far away it is up the string, in other words, where it's vibrating on the string. And these places where the string vibrates are fixed. They are a naturally occurring phenomenon. They are preordained. Man did not create it. Again, the closer the overtone is to the fundamental tone, the stronger the relationship. The fundamental tone generates life, and the life it generates then reflects the importance of the fundamental tone by vibrating in harmony with it.

I know from sitting through college music theory class for two years that I may have lost a few folks here. But don't feel intimidated by the information. I didn't learn a lot of this until I was in college majoring in music. Keep reading and it will become clearer. Or if need be, reread the previous few paragraphs before going on.

FREQUENCY

It's worth repeating that *frequency* means how many times per second a string is vibrating; the higher the number, or the more *frequent* the string vibrates per second, the higher the pitch; the lower the number, or the less *frequent* the string vibrates per second, the lower the pitch. If you've ever gone to a symphony orchestra concert, the first thing you hear when the concert master takes the stage is the orchestra tuning to make sure they're all playing *in tune* with one another. The oboe sounds the note A. This isn't just any A. It's A 440. It's the A that's cycling at 440 beats per second. It's the A that sits around the middle range of most instruments. On the piano it's the A just below middle C.

BUILDING OVERTONES IN THE KEY OF C

Now let's return to the overtone series and build one set using the simplest of notes, the key of C. That means the string that's vibrating is a certain length and a certain width, stretched to a certain tension, and when it's plucked or hammered, it produces a sound of a certain frequency that's called C. Now, let's build the string's overtones. The first overtone is where the string is vibrating at the half. That would make the first overtone C an octave higher, or the ratio of two to one.

The next overtone is where the string is vibrating at the third of the string. And this is where we get our very important interval of the fifth, the interval at the center of our musical mystery. Not only is the fifth the second strongest overtone but it is the first overtone that's *different* from the fundamental tone. In the key of C, the fifth would be the note G. It is an interval of five notes from C, where C is counted as the first note.

I'm going to come back to the fifth in a bit, but before that, let's complete these first few overtones.

The next overtone after the fifth is another C, two octaves above the fundamental tone of C. The next overtone after that is E, a note that is the interval of the third, which is important in the building of chords. The next overtone after that is another G, another fifth but an octave above the first one.

The Fifth Is Perfect and Dominates

Let's concentrate now on the interval of the fifth. Remember, Pythagoras said the most consonant intervals, the ones our ears find pleasing, are the octave, the fourth, and the fifth. Remember that the fifth is the first overtone that is different from the fundamental tone. There's a strong bond generated by the close proximity of the fifth to the fundamental tone by its close mathematical ratio to it. Pythagoras called it a perfect interval. Today music theory students all over the world call it a perfect fifth.

The interval of the fifth is so powerful it dominates the musical landscape. And therefore in music theory it's called the dominant. It has the strongest relationship to the fundamental tone of any note, owing to its close proximity to the fundamental tone in the overtone series. It aids in the establishing of the tonal center. Its presence in a piece of music from the simplest songs to a grand symphony creates this feeling in our ears and in our bodies of coming home, of resolution. The interval of the perfect fifth leads you there by glorifying the foundational tone. The dominant does not glorify itself. It glorifies the tonic, the fundamental tone that gave it life, and in so doing, is glorified as well. For that reason, one could say that the dominant, or perfect fifth, is the Holy Spirit in music. Its purpose is to glorify the source of life, constantly bringing our ears back to the tonic, to the harmonic center.

The Holy Spirit in the Trinity, though, is not created, as it is part of the uncreated godhead. But you can begin to see how this relationship between the dominant and tonic—how the dominant is constantly directing our ear toward home—is much like the Holy Spirit giving us the desire to be home with God, to worship him and him only. Remember our journey? Covenant, sacrifice, glory.

Music itself, the naturally occurring overtones and string ratios, are by themselves morally neutral. But you can see now that whatever subject, person, or idea is put to music will be glorified.

So far we've only been working in the key of C. But all notes work from the same rules. Each fundamental tone generates its own overtone series, with the same relationship of dominant to tonic.

THEOLOGY IN MUSIC: SEVEN, TWELVE, AND FIVE

In the Judeo-Christian faith, certain numbers play a central role in the biblical narrative. In music, numbers do as well. And it's interesting that certain biblical numbers and music theory numbers coincide in importance. For instance, the number seven is the heavenly number. It is the number of days in the account of creation. It is also the number of angels in the apocalyptic book of Revelation, and the number of churches in early Christianity.

In music, seven is the number of notes in the modern notation system: A, B, C, D, E, F, G.

The seven-note scale is the basis of the Western tonal system. You might be familiar with the scale system if you've ever seen the movie *The Sound of Music* and heard one of its most popular songs, "Do Re Mi." It explains the seven-note scale through what's called solfège, which describes the different tones of the seven-note scale.

No doubt Rodgers and Hammerstein drew from their music school training in composing this tune. The order of the seven-note scale—do, re, mi, fa, so, la, ti—is a formula, like a rudimentary bar code. This bar code is made of intervals, of half steps and whole steps in sequence. Start with "one," called the *keynote* or *tonic*. Then we plug in the formula.

Keynote, 1, 1, 1/2, 1, 1, 1, 1/2.

Keynote, whole step, whole step, half step, whole step, whole step, whole step, half step.

Assign this formula anywhere you start on the piano, violin, French horn, or any other instrument, and you will play a major scale.

THE SCALE AND THE LIGHTHOUSE

I see in the scale a musical representation of the lighthouse, as it is itself a physical messenger of God's laws laid out in the Ten Commandments. The light of the lighthouse is its reason for being. It's what defines it. In a musical scale, each one of the notes in the scale is defined first by its relationship to the keynote, and second by its relationship to the other notes in the scale. Let me say this again. Each note in the scale is defined first by its relationship to the keynote or tonic. Just as in the Ten Commandments, each command is defined first by its relationship to the first commandment, "I am the LORD your God. . . . You shall have no other gods before me" (Ex. 20:2–3), and second by their relationship to the other laws. A note's position in the scale is determined by the interval or distance it is from the keynote. What sets up the tonal center of any key is how each note in the scale relates to the keynote. And remember, it's a relationship that man did not create because it's based on the vibratory nature expressed in the overtone series. Man only fine-tuned the raw sound, ordered it as God has commanded us. The scale is the musical representation of our lighthouse! And the lighthouse is the physical reminder of the Ten Commandments. It's the form of law stated musically. There is a seminal point, the keynote. And each member of the system, in this case the scale, is defined first by its relationship to the seminal point, the keynote, and second by its relationship to the other notes.

TWELVE

The other number that figures largely in the Bible is the number twelve. It is the number of Jacob's sons who become the patriarchs of the twelve tribes of Israel. In the New Testament it is the number of apostles of Jesus. In the book of Daniel, there are two numbers used to reference the number of days in an end-times prophecy: 1,290 days and 1,335 days. In each number, if you add the numbers together, they both equal twelve. 1+2+9+0=12, and 1+3+3+5=12.

Even in our lives twelve is important. It's the number of months in a year and the hours in a day.

The number twelve is huge in music as well. If you take an octave—an eight note spread from C to C or A to A—and count up by half notes (on the piano that would be including the five black keys) it adds up to twelve notes, the seven white keys and the five black keys. Now I know I just said music only uses seven notes, and now I'm talking about twelve. But I'm trying to go slowly and not bring too much too quickly into the discussion.

In music there's a relationship between twelve and five that is even more mysterious and fascinating. And even though five is not a biblical number, its presence in music is a glorifying act that our ears hear and our hearts respond to. Remember, I've started calling the interval of the fifth the Holy Spirit of music. That it's *perfect* and that it *dominates*. It helps establish tonal centers, drawing us back home to where our ears feel grounded. It resolves musical tensions, redeeming dissonant sounds and bringing them to their consonant and pleasant conclusions.

Here's something about the perfect fifth that may astound you. If you start at the note C and keep going up by the interval of the perfect fifth, from C to G, from G to D, from D to A, and so on, you'll be back at C in twelve steps!

Music's Biblical Parallels

By applying biblical language to music, some striking parallels emerge. We humans, made in the image of God, are meant to glorify God. It is, according to the Bible, our purpose in life. We are made in his image, called to glorify him, to worship him and him only.

Music is one of our most powerful tools for glorifying God. And some people, myself included, believe it is the most powerful mechanism for worshipping. It is the raw material of sound, ordered in such a way as to promote human flourishing. For when people are making music, they put down their weapons and come together in perfect harmony.

Whether or not you believe there is a God or are still skeptical of my claims that the perfect fifth is the Holy Spirit of music, there are still facts about music that cannot be denied: the physical nature of string ratios; the overtones that sound as one with the fundamental; the overtones helping establish the foundation of harmony; the harmony based on the nature of the relationships between the degrees of the scale and the strength of their position in the overtone series; how music affects the brain; the history of music's power to create, sustain, and even corrupt cultures. These are all facts about music.

What can't be proven by scientific measurement is music's metaphysical nature. Next I will tell you about an experience I had with a specific piece of music that changed my understanding of music from something that was beautiful to something that was ordained by God.

CHAPTER 10

Messiah: Lessons from a Divine Date with Destiny

SOME PEOPLE ARE TRANSFORMED THROUGH WORDS, some through action, some through time spent with friends. My transformation comes through music. It's how I feel closest to God, how I feel God speaks to me. Even when God spoke to me through that photo of a lighthouse one morning in Cathy's summer place, it came years after he had revealed to me a foundational principle in music, through a mysterious encounter in the country of Ethiopia.

As I said in earlier chapters, I do believe there are places with spiritual powers where God chooses to reveal himself. Ethiopia is where I had an incredible moment of spiritual renewal. It changed everything.

I had traveled to Ethiopia in 2008 with the documentary crew from Fox to follow Abyssinian Baptist Church members on a pilgrimage to the land of their founders, marking the church's bicentennial. Abyssinia is the old name of Ethiopia. The country has a rich, ancient history. The land-locked nation in the Horn of Africa contains the headwaters of the Nile River, the longest stream in the world; it is the land of the Queen of Sheba, the royal ruler the Bible mentions who traveled to Jerusalem to meet King

Solomon to gain his wisdom. It is also the land where Ethiopian legend says the ark of the covenant rests; the ark is the vessel where Moses placed the stone tablets on which God wrote the Ten Commandments.

So the crew and I had traveled to Axum, to the Church of Our Lady of Zion where the ark is supposedly housed. The church is a small chapel surrounded by a high iron gate. The chapel, we were told, is occupied by two priests: one on the inside whose only task is to constantly pray over the ark, and the other who attends to the needs of the priest close to the ark. No one sees him or talks to the inside priest. The closest you could come would be to talk to the attending priest. So that's what we'd planned to do. But before we began the interview, a freakish thing happened. While we were negotiating with the priest about interviewing him on camera, our photographer, a veteran with years of experience in the field, placed the camera and tripod on a solid platform, on even ground. Before starting to film, we suddenly heard a crash. The tripod had given way, and the camera fell to the ground. We thought it was broken for sure. Luckily the camera still seemed to be working, so we did the interview with the priest as he stood behind the iron gate.

We thought we had good material. But when we got back to the hotel to view the tape, it was all blue. None of it was useable.

I was extremely disappointed, but not dismayed, chalking it up to one of those setbacks in news that happens frequently. Besides, we had great material with the Abyssinian church members; the senior minister, Dr. Calvin Butts; and the Ethiopian Orthodox Church. So instead of mulling over lost opportunities, back in my hotel room in Addis Ababa I began to put some attention toward preparing for a speech I would give a couple of days after my return to the States on the subject of music and faith. The plan for the talk was to feature a deeper understanding of one of the most iconic pieces of music in all of history, the famed "Hallelujah Chorus" from Handel's oratorio, *Messiah*. So part of that preparation included a harmonic analysis of the music. Using much of the information I explained in the previous chapter, a harmonic analysis means to chart a piece of music's chord progressions, themes, and rhythms, to see how the different parts relate to one another.

It's like making a musical map. It lets you see inside the music's machinery, its inner workings, mathematical relationships; its landmarks, peaks, and valleys. It's something music students learn to do to better understand the music they're playing or listening to.

I remember so vividly looking at the "Hallelujah Chorus," studying the intervals between the notes marking each chord so I could get a good fly-over understanding of how the music shaped up harmonically. As I noticed that certain intervals between notes kept popping up in strategic spots, I began to see in this piece of music something that I had never seen before in the hundreds of times I'd listened to it. And it hit me like a bolt of lightning, how similar a scale in music is to God's holy law. In one instant I saw so clearly how a musical scale's construction follows exactly how I'd learned to understand the structure of the Ten Commandments. There's a seminal point, the keynote, that defines the rest of the system. And that keynote is the surrogate for the first commandment, which states, "I am the LORD your God. . . . You shall have no other gods before me." The musical system works exactly like that. It was one of those moments in life when what I knew intellectually came face-to-face with the spiritual reality of God's existence. It was that moment when the frozen coldness of hard facts comes into contact with the blazing fire of spiritual truth. And as always when ice meets fire, things break. And I broke. My knees buckled, my head bowed; the self-quake, and a revelation of light.

As I look back on that day, I realize that my revelatory moment in the hotel came after the encounter at the chapel that supposedly housed the ark of the covenant, with the priest guarding the gates and the mystery of the damaged camera. Were the day's events related? I cannot say they were. It would be several years later that God revealed to me the connection to the lighthouse.

All I know is at that moment I saw for the first time in the "Hallelujah Chorus" its divinity and the purpose for all music. That realization made me weep. It drenched me with the overwhelming feeling that this particular piece of music was not just divinely inspired, it was divinely ordained. In that moment I was certain that God had smiled on George Frideric Handel and given him the task of setting his gospel to music in a way no other composer in the history of music had ever done or could do. And here, staring me in the face, was its climax, its grandest pinnacle: the redemption of mankind, God's victory.

A Revelation

It was not long after this revelation that I remembered what I'd learned long ago about Handel when he composed the "Hallelujah Chorus." I thought the story to be an urban legend, and many still say that. But from my own experience, I realized that it had to be true. And at least one person confirmed it to me: a musicologist who wrote a book on the spiritual lives of great composers, Dr. Patrick Kavanaugh. He's the director of the Christian Performing Arts Fellowship, whom I interviewed for a Fox Christmas special. In his book is written the story I had been told by my music professor long ago. The story goes that while Handel was holed up in his study composing the three-hour oratorio, he barely ate or slept. While at the very moment he was laying down the words and music to the "Hallelujah Chorus," his servant came into the room. Here's what Dr. Kavanaugh wrote: "The startled composer, tears streaming down his face, turns to this servant and cries out, 'I did think I did see all Heaven before me, and the great God Himself.'"[1]

That is how I felt looking at the music, seeing its structure, delving into its scaffolding and connective tissues. This music, although built by human hands, was very much alive with the soul of almighty God.

Dr. Kavanaugh was gracious enough to sign my copy of his book, and under his signature he wrote, Matt. 5:16: ". . . let your light shine before others, so that they may see your good works and give glory to your Father in Heaven."

I looked up that verse long after I began work on this book, after its title was chosen, its outline and thesis thoroughly organized. Dr. Kavanaugh had chosen a verse to give to me that became a prophetic prediction of what this book would be about: God's light and his glory.

BROKENNESS AND GOD'S PLAN: MESSIAH

While the divinity of Handel's *Messiah* is what helped transform my understanding of God, it was the story of Handel's own life that gave me strength in God's divine providence and grace.

The story of Handel composing this magnificent piece was a reality to me of God's promise that when we are weak, he is strong. When we give up the pretense of being in charge and in control, God does his most amazing work. And I saw in Handel's life a lighthouse experience just as my own, of God revealing himself. Just as in my life, God had taken what was broken and restored it back to life in such a way that there would be no other explanation other than God's divine plan.

Let me explain.

Handel was quite a popular composer in London. He was by all accounts the equivalent of a rock star. But like so many times in life, fortunes change. Other music became the rage, and audiences found a new muse to entice their fancy. Handel faced a waning career. His finances were weak, as was his health, having suffered a stroke. By 1741, at the age of fifty-six, Handel was a broken man at the lowest juncture of his life. The story goes that one evening he was out for a stroll, and one can presume that he was pondering where his life was headed. When he returned, he found something on his doorstep, placed there by a friend of his named Charles Jennens, a wealthy landowner and an amateur musician. It was a libretto, the words for a proposed musical composition. The title on the front page was one word: *Messiah.*

In that one word was contained the answer to all Handel's prayers. *Messiah* would not only be the name of his most famous musical work, but also the source for his personal redemption.

Jennens had compiled the words of *Messiah* from verses of the King James Version of the holy Scriptures, forming what could be called a cliff-note version of the Bible's narrative: of humanity's sinful nature that has separated us from God and of God's loving solution to the problem; the predictions of the prophet Isaiah, of the coming of a messiah; the soothing promises of the Psalms, love songs to God's holiness; the life of Christ in the Gospels of the New Testament; many of the epistles, letters to the early Christian churches; and of course the final chapter, Revelation, God's final triumph. All are condensed to present what is God's plan for the redemption of mankind, of fixing the gift that was broken.

In three short weeks Handel composed the massive three-hour oratorio for orchestra, choir, and soloists. A spiritual and vocational triumph for a man wracked with physical brokenness that challenged his spiritual faith in God.

My Own Brokenness

Handel's story has been an incredible source of inspiration for me as I've gotten older. Although my faith continues to grow, I am constantly challenged by the brokenness in my own body.

I hadn't anticipated getting arthritis. I hadn't planned on my later years being crippled by painful movement of my knees and hips. I also hadn't planned on dystonia in my hand, a nerve issue that affects my ability to play the piano, or the floaters and flashes in my eyes that mar my vision. These things were never part of my dreams of the future. All my life I had been physically active, doing flips in the backyard, cartwheels, splits, and jumping. I took gymnastics lessons and later dance lessons, all the while continuing to play the piano. I felt I could accomplish anything I set my mind to. I realize now that my belief in God was about the hope I'd placed in my future accomplishments, my fitness and drive to make them become a reality. I believed God would provide the path. In other words, my love for and faith in God was more a child's affections for a favorite toy; beloved, cherished, and protected, but never a rock or a refuge. My prayers were more like a spiritual game of "Let's make a deal." Prayers went something like this, in some shape or form: "Oh God, please make him love me. Oh Lord, please help me win the pageant. Oh, dear God, don't let anything happen to my dad."

The prayers were a pleading and heart-wrenching, tear-infused sessions where I had come to a point of desperation, and it was my last-ditch effort to control God. Now I see that so much of my hope was not in God alone, but in the things I was pleading to God for.

Today, I can clearly see that through my physical brokenness, my spiritual brokenness is exposed. Now that I have more years behind than I have ahead of me, there's a resolve to accept this brokenness as a tool that has brought me closer to God. No more can my hope be placed in future goals, because there are not enough years remaining for me. I will never become the next Vladimir Horowitz. I can never be Miss America. I cannot give birth to or raise the five to eight children I'd dreamed about. Letting go of dreams is a painful thing. Seeing many of them dashed on the rocks of life's realities, I can almost understand the pagan sacrifices of ancient times, a timeless Faustian mind-set that makes a deal with any devil or false god to gain what you believe will save you from all harm. Blinded by the darkness of obtaining your heart's desires, you really only have two choices of action: turn from God and become bitter, or turn *to* God and be blessed.

Thanks be to God who gives us the victory through our Lord, Jesus Christ. God is always reaching for us. And he never, ever will abandon those who seek him. A prayer that I continue to pray today that I believe has kept God present and active in my life is, "God, please love me more than I love myself. And let your will rule my life."

Throughout the years of this prayer, God has strengthened me through encounters with people whose physical brokenness brought them to a closer relationship with God. God through Jesus Christ used their brokenness to bring about this incredible spiritual victory. Joni Eareckson Tada, who became a quadriplegic after a diving accident at eighteen years old in 1967, went from being depressed and suicidal to becoming an author, painter, and advocate for the disabled through her ministry Joni and Friends. She is one of the happiest people I've ever met. She laughs with such joy.

That also describes Nick Vujicic. Born without arms or legs, he had a hard early childhood. He also tried to commit suicide, but his life was turned around because the gospel became a reality to him. He travels the world, telling people that "we are all wonderfully and fearfully made from

God." He made me weep with repentance and ask God to forgive my petty wants. These are two people whose physical conditions, which to others seem like profound disadvantages, brought them to a place where they found God as a powerful reality, not as an affable uncle or a benign spirit, but the mighty God, everlasting Father, and Prince of Peace. Their circumstances did not take hope away, but was the driving force that brought their real purpose in life to light.

Their brokenness, Handel's brokenness, and mine, too, was God breaking down the clay, reshaping the material, until finally like Moses in the desert and Jonah in the belly of the whale, "the material was ready for the Maker's hand," to mold it finally into what we are intended to be.[2]

A MISSION

In that hotel room after falling to my knees in tears, I realized that it wasn't information to keep to myself. I had to tell the world. I had to let others know that this music's divine message was for all people, for all time. Its composition came at a time in history when the raw sound of music had been ordered most powerfully, the golden era of the Baroque period. And written by a man whose own brokenness was used as God's holy weapon.

Handel learned what his contemporary Johann Sebastian Bach had always known. That music is meant to praise God. At the end of the score to *Messiah*, he wrote these words: "*Soli Deo Gloria*—To God alone be glory."[3]

I, too, now see that the "Hallelujah Chorus" is no tune to be bastardized to help advertisers sell their products. It's not the punch line in a comedy skit. It is God's victorious anthem, of how he has battled and defeated our enemy, Satan, through putting on flesh and taking the punishment that we deserved. And by so doing began to heal the brokenness in us and in the world.

Perhaps we should all heed the words of Johann Sebastian Bach, in understanding why music has such power over us. He said, "The aim and final end of all music should be none other than the glory of God and the refreshment of the soul."[4]

CONCLUSION

The Power of Three

The foundation has been laid. The garden has been planted.
The musical score written . . . Our task is now to build
the house, to tend the garden, to pay the score.

—N. T. WRIGHT, *THE CHALLENGE OF JESUS*

I CANNOT THINK OF MORE PROPHETIC WORDS TO begin the conclusion to this book than those above of N. T. Wright. He has succinctly summed up the three parts of our world in which we live and about which this book has tried to interpret in the light of the holy Trinity. We live in a world created by God's laws that direct what we build, how we grow, and what we praise and worship through the songs of our hearts. They are seamlessly intertwined in the narrative of our lives, and they are intricately placed in the very workings of our universe.

I have tried in this book to show how the three persons of the holy Trinity (God the Father, God the Son, and God the Holy Spirit) can be our guides, functioning separately as the covenant, the sacrifice, and the glory. But together they weave a powerful fabric, bound in a unity of three forces, hidden in plain sight, in an effortless coexistence.

There have been many times when I have not felt God's presence in my life. Despair or hardship has kept my heart from praising him. But it's at those moments that, apart from my feelings, knowledge of God through his covenants reassures me that God is indeed all around and has not forsaken me. All I need to do is peer at a building or structure and see the power of the cross; to know that both the buildings and I are standing and grounded to this earth because of the reality of the Pythagorean theorem. And this fact testifies to God's covenant of the law of gravity. It is a truth that speaks of the knowledge of God, what can be known. My mind can grasp facts as weapons against errant feelings.

When troubles come, and they will, I can have confidence that whatever I must suffer, the power of resurrection before me every day through the growing of plants and the turn of the seasons, testifies that God will always make a way out of what seems impassable, to bring new life. And that the blood of a resurrected Savior reaches and flows to wherever I am, and that there's power in that blood to move mountains, because it is the same divine blood that created the world.

And when I get angry and lash out at others, turn the anger inward, or become petulant and prideful, I can ask myself, "Who or what are you really worshipping now? To whom are you really bowing down to?" And then I'll remember to repeat the words of the broken, the humble, and the grateful and say, "Forgive me Father," for "to God alone be the glory."

A Final Plea

Perhaps you're not as convinced as I that Christianity is a universal truth for all people for all time. And I can certainly respect that. God gives us all freedom to believe in him as we see fit, or to turn away from him and live out our days in total apathy toward him, or even outright disbelief. I asked a friend once, "Can we live without God?" Her answer, "Yes, because God allows it." God allows us to live without worshipping him, without praising him, even without believing he exists, because that's the nature of true love.

True love does not coerce, cajole, or force itself on to a receiver. Love must be freely given or else it is not love. It is something else. It is any number of other things: fear, selfishness, or pride, masquerading as something noble.

What convinced me that God is real and Christianity true was when I learned what religion actually is. That is one advantage of being a religion correspondent: you have to do at least a little homework on the nature of the thing you cover. At the end of the day all religions, all belief systems offer some sort of salvation. It's a formula. Here's how it works. There's a set of principles, practices, or rituals that say, "Do *this* and you will achieve *that*." And the "that" is usually happiness, nirvana, peace, heaven, or rightness with the deity of choice. But Christianity is the only religion that says you can't earn your salvation. The work of saving has already been accomplished. Instead of myriad ways of trying to reach God and never knowing if we're good enough, Christianity says, no, God has been reaching for us; he stood in the gap, in the eternal chasm created by Adam between sinful humanity and himself and endured the judgment of his own wrath. All we need to do is believe in the One who did the work, Jesus Christ, the Logos, God made flesh. We are good not to get something, but because of what we've been given.

But let's go back to that simple formula for religion: "Do this and you will get that." You can see how this equation is a means through which anything can become a source of salvation. First we identify the thing we believe will give our lives the desired meaning and make a covenant with it. It can be anything or a combination of things, like career, beauty, success, being smarter than anyone else, being wealthier. And most of us don't even realize with what we've made a covenant.

Second, we learn to sacrifice to that thing we've made a covenant with. We give up our time and sometimes the quality of our relationships in order to have the thing we've made a covenant with.

Third, we must justify our sacrifices by strengthening the bond with the thing that we've made a covenant with. It's the act of worship.

Here's the pattern in real life. I've taken these examples right from the pages of the news, and I'm interpreting them, for the most part, without speaking directly to the people involved. So in all honesty it's my interpretation. You can agree or disagree, but it makes the most sense to me, and you'll have to decide for yourself.

The saddest stories I cover in the news business or read about, are those of suicides. It absolutely breaks my heart hearing of anyone who is in such despair as to think that taking his or her own life is the only way out. There was one story of a woman who took her life because she suffered greatly from a rare form of a disease that was intensely painful. And then I read of a man who suffered from the same illness, who wrote that despite his pain, killing himself was not the answer. I was struck by his sincerity and faith, so I reached out to him to find out more about how he could endure the hardship of excruciating pain. He told me that when he put his faith in the living God, he was able to see a whole new purpose for his life. He said when he did that, he lived longer than his doctors thought he would. And because of it he was able to offer hope and healing to the people around him. We also talked about the nature of suicide, and I told him it sounded like he thought of suicide as a form of sacrifice to a false idol. And he agreed wholeheartedly.

I began to look at all suicides in the news differently, of how, perhaps, they all could be thought of in that way—a sacrifice to a false god. Just recently reports have surfaced about the dramatic rise in the number of suicides nationwide. It has baffled the medical industry. But, perhaps, another increase in another area could offer some clues. You see, paralleling the rise in suicides, there's also been a rise in the number of people who proclaim no faith. They're what is called "the nones." They have no religious affiliation to organized religion. They often self-identify as "spiritual but not religious."

Are these two things related? I hope to explore this idea in subsequent writings because I think it's too serious an issue to try to fully explain here. But if this fact is true, that we don't have a choice of whether to worship but what we worship, and if we're not living out the doctrines of Truth found in the holy Scriptures, then we will look to anything to give us a reason for living. And that reason can be health, wealth, success, relationships, approval, or any combination of good things we strive for in our lives. But if those things become ultimate things, our reason for living, they become idols. They become the things we make covenants to. And when we fail to live up to their demands—if we lose a job, a relationship, money, etc.—it is as if we have failed our false idol's commands. We have violated the rules. We have sinned. And the penalty for sin is death. That is God's Law, his truth for this world that we cannot escape (Rom. 6:23). It is written in Scripture but also in nature, which includes us. And that is why God warns incessantly against worshipping false gods. It is not to spoil our fun, but to save our lives! And not just to save us from death, but from despair and depression, which are forms of a living death.

There's the other part of that verse in Romans that gives us assurances that no false idol can. And that is God has paid the penalty for sin. It is his "gift" to us. Jesus on the cross paid the penalty for sin. He died so that we won't have to. This is how he fixed the original gift that was broken.

Another story that is more focused on a global trend showed how the declining birthrate is jeopardizing a nation's future as there are fewer babies being born than can help support an aging generation. The cycle of life has a hitch in it. The reason given in the article was "because of a growing 'decadence,' in which people live for their own pleasure, 'while shrugging off the basic sacrifices that built our civilization in the first place.'"[1]

Here we have a worldwide phenomenon of several generations of people who have made a covenant with individual freedom and self-expression. Instead of them making sacrifices to bring new life into the world, it creates a scenario by which other generations must be sacrificed. And the culture's collective praise of such freedoms strengthens the bond. The nature of sacrifice has only two paths: one says, "My life given for yours," the other, "Your life given for me." This story of a declining birthrate shows how lack of sacrifice can operate on a global level in addition to one-on-one relationships.

Now let me tell you of a more positive example of faith at work. A story from last year heralded that Israel was set to honor an American World War II soldier. Master Sergeant Roddie Edmonds had been "the top non-commissioned officer in a German POW camp in January of 1945 when the order came down for Jewish-American captives to step forward." Edmonds answered, "We are all Jews here." Even when "the German officer pressed a Luger to Edmonds'[s] head, Edmonds wouldn't budge." The article goes on quoting Edmonds's son the Rev. Chris Edmonds, "And then my dad said, 'If you are going to shoot, you are going to have to shoot all of us because we know who you are and you'll be tried for war crimes when we win this war.'" It's estimated that on that day Edmonds "saved the lives of more than 200 Jewish-American soldiers."[2]

Roddie Edmonds had made a covenant with the real God of the universe and was willing to sacrifice his own life to save others, to stand in the breach between life and certain death, just as his Savior had. Edmonds's life was a testament to his worship of God.

These are three stories, vignettes from three scenarios. But we all have a story, a narrative depicting our struggles, triumphs, and failures. All of the twists and turns, plots and subplots, have had a hand in writing the story of our lives. And at the end of the day, our stories are about our relationships. Relationships with the people in our lives, of course, but more broadly, interactions with the world in which we live. We are protagonists in our own stories as we discover how we fit in to our family, with our friends, in our community, and finally in the world at large.

But God also has a story. It's just one story. How he created the world, made choices laying down the precepts of how it should be built, how it should grow, and how all things would testify to its Author. And the Bible is constantly telling us about it. In Romans, for example, "For since the creation of the world God's invisible qualities—his eternal power and divine nature—have been clearly seen, being understood from what has been made" (1:20).

The gospel of Jesus Christ contained in the holy Scriptures is a living and breathing document. It gives life. It transforms life. It sustains life. The covenant of laws is about choices we make in life—because God himself made choices when he created the world, when he made the laws. And then those choices are transformed into actions and reactions. How we react determines how we grow. Some actions draw us closer to God, other actions away from God.

What I am so grateful for is that the gospel of Jesus Christ allowed me to gently replace the faulted template of my own story with the true pattern set down by God. He showed me the light of the gospel through a tiny, framed old photo of a lighthouse. Its power penetrated all that I am and helped me to experience the living and breathing gospel, transforming my life into what I was meant to be, a child of the living God, loved and precious to him. God upgraded my system with an eternal application that will never need replacing.

Now I've learned to look at everything—every relationship, every situation—through the light of God's guidance. By his light I see light.

Is There Power in Three?

But, perhaps you're not convinced that it's possible to narrow down the world to three parts; perhaps the world is so incredibly complicated and multifaceted that it cannot be whittled to so few. Well, I think it can, and here's why.

In the Bible, the number three pops up with extraordinary regularity, as either a number of days, a number of people, or a number of events. When Jews referred to their God, it was the God of Abraham, Isaac, and Jacob, the three patriarchs of their lineage as God's chosen people. When Abraham journeyed to sacrifice his son Isaac, he arrived at the place on the third day. When Jacob's favored son Joseph was thrown in jail and interpreted the dreams of Pharaoh's baker and cupbearer, each of their dreams involved three things: the cupbearer saw a vine with three branches, the baker dreamt of three baskets of bread. Joseph understood that each meant three days time would pass before their sentences would be carried out.

When Moses went to Pharaoh to demand he let the Israelites go, he asked, "Let us take a three-day journey into the wilderness to offer sacrifices to the LORD our God" (Ex. 3:18).

Jonah was in the belly of the whale for three days.

In the New Testament, the significance continues with the three wise men's three gifts to the newborn King.

Three is the number of times Satan tempted Jesus in the wilderness, it is the number of times Peter denied Jesus, and the number of times he proclaimed his love for Jesus after the resurrection.

There are many more references to the number three in the Bible; all, I believe, are a foreshadowing of the greatest event the whole story of the Bible is about: Jesus was crucified, laid in a tomb, and on the third day he rose from the grave.

The importance of three as a number is not confined to Christianity and Judaism. It's also important in Buddhism, Hinduism, and Taoism.

In mathematics it is the smallest odd prime number. In architecture it's the number of elements needed to determine spatial dimensions: height, width, depth, and the least number of legs to hold up a chair or structure.

The trinitarian concept pervades our world. And so it is not even a leap of faith; it could be considered a divine directive to create a world using only these three unified parts of Father, Son, and Holy Spirit. It is the state of all things; relationships are woven into the fabric of creation, each thread as a purpose, binding us to the Creator, letting us take part in his grand design. Ravi Zacharias put it, "How does one find unity in diversity when both are realities? The answer is that unity and diversity exist in the created order because unity and diversity exist in the community of the Trinity, the first cause."[3]

But each thread is anchored in love. Love that's so amazing it created this world. Love that is so binding it sustains this world. And love that is so constant and unwavering that it will redeem this world.

Love so amazing and so divine that it took the punishment of its own wrath in order for us to be reconciled and transformed. It's a gift that we cannot possibly return in kind. God loves because God is love. He loves us not because we deserve it, but because that is God's nature.

We live in a world that God created. Everything in it bares his mark. We can no more escape from God than a zebra can run from his stripes.

God's love is what binds this world. It is the light of this world. And it is the only reality we need.

Ask yourself these questions:

- What have I made a covenant with in my life?
- What am I sacrificing for that covenant?
- In what ways am I worshipping what has been built?

In the words of Joshua, it is a daily opportunity to say, "Choose for yourselves this day whom you will serve." And to state boldly the only plausible solution: "As for me and my household, we will serve the LORD" (Josh. 24:15).

A Small Lesson in Music History and a Harmonic Analysis of the "Hallelujah Chorus"

As I mentioned in chapter 9, there is hardly an entity in this world that is more a combination of law and love than music. The strictness by which music is created is based on its physical nature. The physics of music is based on its mathematical vibrations, as on a violin, a piano string, or a trumpet blast's oscillating sound waves. But I believe and still maintain that music's emotional impact on our souls is born of one note that dominates. That note is called the perfect fifth, the fifth degree of a seven-note scale. The note's power comes from its position in the overtone series. And it dominates not by glorifying itself, but by glorifying the thing that gives it life. It's what I've called the Holy Spirit of music.

Western classical music has several different styles based on the era in which the music was written. But it's all based on a notation system that's only been around for a few hundred years. George Frideric Handel and his contemporary Johann Sebastian Bach were composing in what's called the Baroque period of the early seventeenth and mid-eighteenth centuries. It's a style of music that is sometimes called the Golden Age of classical music because of its strict adherence to the rules of counterpoint. This strict adherence to counterpoint is why the music of Bach sounds different from the music of Russian composer Sergei Rachmaninoff, who lived more than two hundred years later.

Counterpoint is important to understand because it helps explain how Western music harnessed the power of the perfect fifth. After the first few overtones the mathematical relations between the notes are no longer exact. They exist in odd numerical ratios. Before the Baroque period, this limited the number of musicians who could play together or the intervals and the types of chords they could play together because the sound would be too dissonant, or unpleasant. In the early Baroque period, musicians began doing something that corrected this problem. They developed what's called a tempering of the notes. They made it so that the notes were equidistant apart. And when they did this, it meant the notes' mathematical relations, based on their overtones, were much more in sync and closely aligned.

Here's an example. Remember how the perfect fifth—or dominant—is the fifth degree of the seven-note scale? That means going from left to right starting at the keynote, let's say C, it's five steps, which would be the note G. And G in the key of C is the dominant, the Holy Spirit of that key. If you start on the same keynote C and go right to left to the G directly below C, the actual distance is the interval of a fourth. But because you'd still be in the tonality of the key of C, it's still recognized as the dominant even though the actual distance is the interval of the fourth. And it's one of the reasons the fourth interval is also called perfect. But wait. The perfect fourth in the key of C is F. That is why even music students get confused, because in the key of F, the dominant is C. That means that in the key of F, the note C is five steps away from F on a seven-note scale.

You may now begin to see that by tempering the distance between the notes, their mathematical relationships are now working with, not against one another. As I explain further it will sound a great deal like an algebra equation, which is why it's been said that music is mathematics for the soul.

If C is the dominant of F and G the dominant of C, then if you want to smoothly change keys or modulate from key to key, say, move from the key of G to the key of F, you use their common strength: the note C. It is the dominant of F and the sub-dominant of G. Using C allows for a seamless switch to a new tonality. Your ear hears a pleasant progression, but your body feels heightened emotion.

Pop music icon Barry Manilow was famous for modulating his songs, creating greater emotional impact. Well, he can credit the musical geniuses of the early Baroque period for that. They harnessed the power of the perfect fifth through this ordering or tempering of the scales and created strict rules as to how the notes should fit together.

These strict rules were called counterpoint, a set of guidelines that keeps the relationship between notes pure, in a sense, dictating how notes should travel *to* and *from* each other. As time progressed, composers began to step out of those strict rules. You can hear the changes in the music throughout history as we pass through the Baroque period to the Classical period[1] of Mozart and Beethoven and their contemporaries, then to the Romantic period typified by composers like Johannes Brahms and Frédéric Chopin. Each period of music gets further and further away from the strict counterpoint, but they never quite leave it altogether. Counterpoint is still the base over which the music is operating, and the relationship between the dominant—the fifth degree or note of the scale—and the tonic—the first degree or note—is the crucial element. You can hear the power of the perfect fifth, the dominant in nearly all music today, whether it's a hymn or a top-ten hit, "Mary Had a Little Lamb" or "Proud Mary," a symphony or a soulful ballad.

During the golden age of music, the Baroque period, one composer almost defines the era. It's the German, J. S. Bach, who some historians consider to be the greatest composer who ever lived. He was a church organist and composed music almost exclusively for the praising of God. He would routinely write at the end of his scores *Soli Deo Gloria*, "To God alone, the glory." His fellow German was the composer George Frideric Handel, who also loomed large. Born the same year as Bach, in 1685, he was also rather religious, but his musical path in life was different from his countryman. He didn't compose primarily for the church but for the stage. He traveled outside of Germany, settled in England, and became the toast of London society. But unbeknownst to Handel, his life in his adoptive homeland would culminate in what was a divine date with destiny.

I cannot in this space do a complete exegesis of *Messiah*. But I can and will now explore the one piece whose musical confluence of law and love came to me in a revelation one evening in that hotel room in Ethiopia. *Hallelujah!*

DIVINE HARMONY BEHIND THE "HALLELUJAH CHORUS"

The words alone to the "Hallelujah Chorus" are powerful. All of them are taken from the Bible's last book, the apocalyptic book of Revelation.

Alleluia: for the Lord God omnipotent reigneth. (19:6 KJV)

The kingdoms of this world are become the kingdoms of our Lord,
and of his Christ; and he shall reign for ever and ever. (11:15 KJV)

KING OF KINGS, AND LORD OF LORDS. (19:16 KJV)

Hallelujah!

I first heard a performance of *Messiah* live when I was a teenager working as an usher at Orchestra Hall in Minneapolis. But before that I was introduced to the entire oratorio while at a summer four-week music camp called the High School Musicians Project at the University of Minnesota. *Messiah* is such a landmark piece in the landscape of musical history that the professor there, Dr. Vern Sutton, thought it important enough that we begin to study its inner workings even as high school musicians. I know now that that experience was God planting a seed in me that one day would blossom into a full-blown understanding of this music's impact on the world.

One of the things I remember so vividly about the class is the explanation of something called word painting. That's a musical device where the notes mimic what the words are saying. In the chorus of "All We Like Sheep," the words "have gone astray" are painted musically by the notes on the word *astray*, literally sounding like they've lost their way. The chorus goes on and on, twisting and turning, giving the impression they are wandering aimlessly. In the tenor aria "Every Valley," when the tenor sings the phrase, "Every valley shall be exalted," the notes go up; when he sings the words, "Every mountain shall be made low," the notes go down; and when he sings, "The rough places made plain," the music stays even. There are loads of examples like this throughout the entire oratorio, and just understanding this made a huge impression on me that transformed me from a kid who played the piano to a serious musician.

But it took more than three decades for me to have my most profound moment with *Messiah*. I will now take you through what I found in the harmonic analysis of the "Hallelujah Chorus" to show how the music speaks the words on the paper.

Hallelujah!

The word *hallelujah* or *alleluia* means "praise the Lord." It's made up of two Hebrew words, *hallel*, which means "praise," and *Yah*, for "Yahweh" or "Jehovah," the word for God. The "Hallelujah Chorus" is a choral work created for the sole purpose of praising God for what he has done, for his victory.

The first two things I did in the harmonic analysis was to figure out first its key and then its meter or rhythm. The "Hallelujah Chorus" is in 4/4 time. That means there are four quarter notes per measure with the emphasis on the first and third beats. Count to yourself four even beats: 1, 2, 3, 4. Now count again emphasizing the first and third beats without slowing down or speeding up. *1*, **2**, *3*, **4**. It should feel like a march. That is the basic meter of the "Hallelujah Chorus."

Now to the key signature; Handel chose the key of D major to present this triumphal piece because the composers of his time believed certain keys embodied certain characteristics and exuded certain emotions. The key of C major, for instance, was the key of innocence and simplicity; a lot of children's songs are composed in this key. The key of F minor (generally speaking, minor sounds sad, major sounds happy) was thought to be the key of "deep depression and a longing for the grave." While the key of G major expressed "true friendship and faithful love."[2]

The key of D major was thought to be the triumphal key. And not just any triumph, but of a triumph in battle, a victory cry after a great war has been waged and won. It is the key of heaven rejoicing.

Today, though, we don't as easily see emotions tied to specific keys. Songs are transposed to fit a singer's range. When I played keyboards in the Little Rockers band for the *Huckabee Show*, I had to transpose songs into other keys depending on if the original key was too high or too low for the singer. So even though we don't abide by the characteristics of certain notes today, Handel was influenced by that mode of thinking. And that's what's important.

Knowing the key a song or piece is in tells you something else that's important to understand: the music's tonal center, its seminal point that defines all other relationships in the music. In this case D major. It means the piece begins on the note D and ends on D. The music may move away from D and modulate to closely related keys to develop the themes and heighten emotion, but it will return to D, as a coming home. Your ear hears this without even knowing what it's hearing, but you feel it somewhere deep down in you, this harmonic focus on the home key, the tonal center, in this case D.

It's at this point in my analysis while in that hotel room that the overwhelming revelation hit me. I began to see how similar a scale in music is to God's holy law. In an instant I saw so clearly how a musical scale's construction follows exactly how I'd learned to understand the structure of the Ten Commandments. Just like a lighthouse. There's a light, a seminal point that defines the rest of the system, that is the surrogate for the first commandment, that states, "I am the LORD your God. . . . You shall have no other gods before me" (Ex. 20:2–3). The musical system works exactly like that.

In the "Hallelujah Chorus" these notes are defined first by their relationship to D and second by their relationship to one another. Each note in a D major scale (or any scale) is defined first by its distance from the first note, it's interval from the keynote or tonic.

Here's the scale D, E, F sharp, G, A, B, [D]. If you assign numbers to a seven-note scale, you see, 1, 2, 3, 4, 5, 6, 7, [1].

But the numbers don't tell you the whole story; they don't explain what's happening between those notes. Number two on the scale is not called two just because it comes second, but rather because it's the interval of a major second from the first note. And three, the third note, is not just three, it's a major third from the first note; and the fourth, a perfect fourth from the first note; the fifth, a perfect fifth from the first note; the sixth, a major sixth from the first note; the seventh, a major seventh from the first note. That means that in a piece of music these notes will always maintain that relationship with the keynote. No matter where they pop up in the music, their identities are based on their relationships with that note.

So the "Hallelujah Chorus" begins in the key of D with a short, three-measure instrumental introduction. The choir in full voice sings the triumphal word, *hallelujah*, ten times over eight measures. The first five times *hallelujah* is sung it's in the home key of D major. Then the music makes a quick modulation to the key of A major and then repeats *hallelujah* another five times. This quick move to A is important to understand because A is the dominant of D, it's the Holy Spirit of D. So everything that belongs to the tonality of A is now praising God too. It's as if Handel has stated emphatically in musical language in these opening measures that all praise be unto God by first saying it in the home key, the godlike equivalent. Then he lets the Holy Spirit equivalent, the dominant of A, give voice as well.

Next, all voices and instruments are in unison, presenting the strongest exaltation possible for the next line: unison. Unison occurs when all voices are on the same note in their own ranges, which means they're singing in the strongest interval possible, the octave, the keynote with itself—all say with one voice, "For the Lord God omnipotent reigneth." This line starts on A, the dominant (perfect fifth), and goes up until it lands back on D, the keynote, on the word *God*. Understand that in coming back to the keynote on the word *God*, Handel is leading you back *to* God! He has moved you from the dominant, back to the tonic, taking you musically from the Holy Spirit back to the Father.

Then on the word *omnipotent*, the music jumps an octave, the entirety of a scale, and back, then steps back down to the A on *reigneth*.

What Handel has done in these opening lines is use the music to paint the picture of an omnipotent God who reigns over everything and forever. He has used the breadth of the scale to color your mind with the sound of eternity, the audible presence of a victorious and sovereign God. The words beg for another round of hallelujahs! And so, the choir sings four more, with the chords jumping back and forth from D major to A major. After a repeat of this exchange, the choir finesses these two lines, singing a contrapuntal masterpiece of frenzied "hallelujahs" and "For the Lord God omnipotent reigneth," each choral part taking turns singing the lines, going around, under and over one another; the orchestra underneath doing equally as much. Then suddenly, or *subito*, there is calm.

The music begins its most contemplative moment to introduce the next thought. It is almost a prayer, sung in a hush, in a whisper, but never slowing, which gives it added energy, as if to say, "I can hardly believe it's really true. It's too amazing to grasp." In hard-to-restrain softness, containing an eagerness that wants to explode, the choir sings, "The kingdom of this world is become . . ." It's like all incredible news begins, you tell your closest friends, slowly and deliberately, in even words, but low and measured as you try to impart the greatness of it by the tone of your voice. "You won't believe what has happened!"

And then a fast and furious crescendo creeps in because the news can't be held back, so the choir explodes singing, ". . . the kingdom of our Lord and of His Christ!" And then repeats to emphasize, "And of His Christ."

And now the part that is sure to help you see the divine working behind the pen of Handel: "And He shall reign forever and ever." It sounds like the choir is jumping randomly from note to note on this line, but there's something important happening here. The choir is leaping so that each two notes go from a dominant to the tonic, from a Holy Spirit note, to its corresponding Father-like equivalent. And-he-shall-reign-for-ever, and ever.

"King of kings, and Lord of lords, King of kings and Lord of lords." The music is saying it, as well, as it keeps pushing to the D, the keynote, from the A, it's dominant: A-A-D = King-of-kings; A-A-D = Lord-of-lords; A-A-D = King-of-kings, A-A-D = Lord-of-lords. The timpani, too, pounds in rhythm A-A-D, A-A-D. Heralding the Holy Spirit to God. Dominant to tonic, dominant to tonic, Holy Spirit to God, Holy Spirit to God.

Just when you think the music can reach no higher height, the sopranos take it even higher and sing a high on A the words, "King of kings," and the other parts answer in antiphon, "For ever and ever. Hallelujah, hallelujah." Again the sopranos complete the thought and sing, "And Lord of lords;" another antiphon answer, "For ever and ever. Hallelujah, hallelujah." Then the sopranos begin the sequence again but this time on D. But Handel fools the ear because now we are in the key of A. The sopranos are moving step-like up the A major scale, completing the emotional climax on E, the dominant of A. Now the basses will take that jumping sequence from dominant to tonic, on "And he shall reign for ever and ever," ending on A. But immediately the sopranos follow suit with the same line, starting on the A where the basses ended and continuing the jump from dominant to tonic until we're again back to D. And then the altos, tenors, and basses sing in one strong voice, each in its own part, "King of kings," and hold the last note while the sopranos, now the antiphon, answer, "Forever and ever." Again, the altos, tenors, and basses finish the thought, "And Lord of lords," holding out the last note, over which the angelic voices of the sopranos sing, "Hallelujah, hallelujah." Then the coda begins to take us on this furiously faithful journey toward the conclusion. We are all disciples at this point, and we know where we're headed. We are headed on our journey home to D, home to be with God.

In four-part harmony all sing, "And He shall reign for ever and ever,

King of kings and Lord of lords, King of kings and Lord of lords." The sopranos continue with "King of kings and Lord of lords" while the other voices sing again and again, "For ever and ever, and ever." The news is too incredible, too overwhelming, so all that can be said is, "Hallelujah! Hallelujah! Hallelujah! Hallelujah! Hallelujah!"

On its first performance in London, the power of the "Hallelujah Chorus" made an earthly king rise to his feet to bow to its majesty. King George III was so moved he rose from his seat, recognizing that he was a peasant in the presence of the King of kings. And an entire concert hall audience rose with him. Today the tradition continues. At performances of *Messiah* worldwide, audiences rise to the sound of the "Hallelujah Chorus." King George III may have started the tradition, but for me there's no sitting down when it's time to praise the Lord!

Acknowledgments

I COULD NEVER HAVE WRITTEN THIS BOOK WITHOUT the influence over the years of so many great men and women of faith. It would take another book to thank them all and to explain their roles in my faith journey. But I would like to acknowledge Redeemer Presbyterian Church in New York City and its ministerial staff led by Dr. Timothy Keller. It was through the church's ministry that I began to look at faith in Jesus Christ in a whole different light. Over the past decade plus, I've been intellectually challenged and confronted, while at the same time spiritually nourished and strengthened. I can honestly say that the combination created in me a contentment I had never experienced before in my life; the God-shaped space in my soul finally being filled with the proper materials.

Notes

Introduction: Eye-opening Confessions

1. Hymn, *Amazing Grace,* words by John Newton, published 1779.

Chapter 1: The Lighthouse

1. Kyriacos C. Markides, *The Mountain of Silence: A Search for Orthodox Spirituality* (New York: Crown Publishing Group, 2002), 12.
2. http://www.history.com/images/media/interactives/lighthouses.pdf.
3. Robert Louis Stevenson, Edmund Gosse, and Leslie Stephen, *The Works of Robert Louis Stevenson,* vol. 8 (Scotland: Greenock Press, 1906), 235.
4. Gordon Lightfoot, "The Wreck of the Edmund Fitzgerald," from the album *Summertime Dream,* compact disc, originally released August 1976.
5. Katharina von Schlegel, Jane Borthwick, trans., "Be Still My Soul," *The United Methodist Hymnal #534,* 1989, http://www.hymnary.org/hymn/UMH/534.
6. Gerald O'Collins and Mary Ann Meyers, *Light from Light: Scientists and Theologians in Dialogue* (Grand Rapids: Wm. B. Eerdmans Publishing, 2012), 2.
7. Interview with Dr. Alistir McGrath, Andreas Idreos Professor of Science and Religion at the University of Oxford: March 13, 2012, Oxford, England.
8. Interview with Dr. John Lennox, Christian apologist and Professor of Mathematics at the University of Oxford: March 13, 2012, Oxford, England.
9. Ibid.
10. O. Palmer Robertson, *The Christ of the Covenants* (Grand Rapids: Baker Book House, 1981).

175

11. Leon Kass, *The Beginning of Wisdom: Reading Genesis* (New York: Simon and Schuster, 2003), 16.

Chapter 2: Law Born of Love

1. John Doody, Kevin L. Hughes, and Kim Paffenroth, ed., *Augustine and Politics* (Oxford: Lexington Books, 2005), 152.
2. Richard Leslie Parrott, *The Reluctant Journey: Fulfilling God's Purpose for You* (New York: HarperCollins, 2014), 57.
3. O. Palmer Robertson, *The Christ of the Covenants* (Grand Rapids: Baker Book House, 1981).
4. Larry S. Chapp, *The God of Covenant and Creation* (New York: T&T Clark International, 2011), 24.
5. Elmer A. Martens, *God's Design, Fourth Edition* (Eugene, OR: Wipf and Stock Publishers, 2015), 239.
6. Michael Horton, *Introducing Covenant Theology* (Grand Rapids: Baker Books, 2009), 31.
7. Sarah Knapton, "Bright Flash of Light Marks Incredible Moment Life Begins When Sperm Meets Egg," *The Telegraph*, April 26, 2016, http://www.telegraph.co.uk/science/2016/04/26/bright-flash-of-light-marks-incredible-moment-life-begins-when-s/.

Chapter 3: A House, A Home

1. Sermon by Rev. David Bisgrove, "Home from Exile," Redeemer Presbyterian Church, New York, NY. January 10, 2016.
2. Ibid.
3. Josephus, as quoted in John H. Walton, *The Lost World of Genesis One: Ancient Cosmology and the Origins Debate* (Downers Grove, IL: InterVarsity Press, 2010), 81.
4. "Transcript: The Kalam Cosmological Argument," *Reasonable Faith with Willaim Lane Craig,* accessed August 18, 2016, http://www.reasonablefaith.org/transcript-kalam-cosmological-argument.
5. "Physics," *CERN: Accelerating Science,* accessed August 18, 2016, https://home.cern/about/physics.
6. Interview with Dr. William Lane Craig, Research Professor of Philosophy, Talbot School of Theology: July 10, 2012.
7. Ibid.
8. Interview with author: February, 1, 2012, Washington, D.C.

Chapter 4: A Temple and the Choices We Make

1. Buffalo, NY Diocese, 2004–12, http://www.buffalodiocese.org/st.-joseph -cathedral.

2. Louis Berkhof, *Systematic Theology* (Grand Rapids: Wm. B. Eerdmans Publishing, 1996), 515.

3. Nicholas Pugliese, "Dumont Police Conclude Investigation of Boy's Fatal Jump from Grant School Window," *The Record*, April 1, 2015, http://www. northjersey.com/news/dumont-police-conclude-investigation-of-boy-s-fatal -jump-from-grant-school-window-1.1300247?page=all.

4. Christine Ha, "Moments," *Chinese Christian Mission*, 2006, http://ccmusa.org /read/read.aspx?id=chg20060101.

5. Ibid.

6. Dr. Leslie R. Green, "Darkness to Light Stories: Life Lessons of the Author and Others," a dissertation submitted to the faculty of the graduate school of The University of Minnesota, October 2006.

7. Ibid.

Chapter 5: The Tears, the Blood, the Power

1. Andrae Crouch, "The Blood Will Never Lose Its Power," 1970. Copyright: Lyrics © Sony/ATV Music Publishing, LLC, Kobalt Music Publishing Ltd.

2. Andrew Murray, *The Power of the Blood of Jesus* (New Kensington, PA: Whitaker House, 1993), 63.

3. Edward Insinger, from the shroud of Turin replica testing, 1980s. Currently resides in Summit, NJ.

4. Ibid.

5. Jennifer F. Wilson, Monica Laberge, and Rebecca J. Frey, "Anemias," *The Gale Encyclopedia of Medicine: Science in Context*, 2015, http://ic.galegroup. com/ic/scic/ReferenceDetailsPage/ReferenceDetailsWindow?failOverType =&query=&prodId=SCIC&windowstate=normal&contentModules=&disp lay-query=&mode=view&displayGroupName=Reference&limiter=&currPa ge=&disableHighlighting=false&displayGroups=&sortBy=&search_within _results=&p=SCIC&action=e&catId=&activityType=&scanId=&document Id=GALE%7CXJRABU838537478&source=Bookmark&u=imcpl45551& jsid=cb502caabbe6ce7b0bedbf439ea3c302.

6. Leland Ryken, James C. Wilhoit, and Tremper Longman III, eds., *Dictionary of Biblical Imagery* (Downers Grove, IL: InterVarsity Press, 2010), 100.

7. Interview with Dr. N. T. Wright, New Testament scholar and retired Anglican bishop: March 23, 2012, New York, NY.

8. George Rawlinson, *Phoenicia: History of a Civilization* (New York: I. B. Tauris, 2005), 113.

9. "Child Abuse Statistics and Facts," *Childhelp.org*, 2014, https://www.childhelp .org/child-abuse-statistics/.

Chapter 6: Lessons from the Vineyard

1. Leland Ryken, James C. Wilhoit, and Tremper Longman III, eds., *Dictionary of Biblical Imagery* (Downers Grove, IL: InterVarsity Press, 2010), 596.

2. Ibid.

3. Ibid., 914.

4. Interview with James Silver, General Manager, Peconic Bay Winery: April 6, 2012, Cutchogue, NY.

5. Ibid.

6. Peter H. Raven, Ray F. Evert, and Susan E. Eichhorn, *Biology of Plants* (New York City: Macmillan 2005), 91.

7. Hugh Ross, *The Genesis Question: Scientific Advances and the Accuracy of Genesis* (Carol Stream, IL: NavPress, 2001).

8. Jean Paul Corriveau, *A Personal Journey into the Quantum World: God's Silent World* (Bloomington, IL: iUniverse, 2009), 360.

9. Hugh Ross, *The Genesis Question: Scientific Advances and the Accuracy of Genesis* (Carol Stream, IL: NavPress, 2001), 97.

10. Ibid.

11. Interview with James Silver, General Manager, Peconic Bay Winery: April 6, 2012, Cutchogue, NY.

12. Interview with Dr. David Tukey, Postdoctoral Fellow in Molecular Neurobiology, NYU Medical Center: January 7, 2012, New York, NY.

13. Interview with Dr. Andrew Newberg, Director of Research at the Myrna Brind Center for Integrative Medicine, Thomas Jefferson University: March 27, 2012, Philadelphia, PA.

14. Interview with Dr. Denis Alexander, Director, Farraday Institute for Science and Religion, St. Edmunds College: March 15, 2012, Cambridge, UK.

15. Ibid.

16. Ibid.

17. Ibid.

18. Ibid.

19. Ibid.

Chapter 7: Love Language and Sacrifice

1. Brian A. Wren, "I Come with Joy to Meet My Lord," composed in 1971, revised 1995, Hope Publishing Company, *hymnary.org*, http://www.hymnary .org/text/i_come_with_joy_to_meet_my_lord.
2. A reference to the cartoon character I grew up watching. A big baby who never grew out of wearing diapers.
3. Dr. Timothy Keller, "Love, the Most Excellent Way: Based on 1 Corinthians 13:1–13" (sermon, Redeemer Presbyterian Church, New York City, May 1, 2016).
4. Ibid.
5. Ibid.
6. Stephen D. Krashen, *Explorations in Language Acquisition and Use* (Ontario: Pearson Education Canada, 2003), 4.
7. C. S. Lewis, *The Four Loves* (Boston: Houghton Mifflin Harcourt, 1991), 117.

Chapter 8: The Song of My Soul

1. Fox Butterfield and Constance L. Hays, "A Boston Tragedy: The Stuart Case," *The New York Times*, January 15, 1990, http://www.nytimes.com /1990/01/15/us/boston-tragedy-stuart-case-special-case-motive-remains -mystery-deaths-that-haunt.html?pagewanted=all.
2. Dr. Timothy Keller, *Counterfeit Gods: The Empty Promises of Money, Sex, and Power, and the Only Hope that Matters* (New York: Penguin Books, 2009).
3. Shawn Cohen, Frank Rosario, and Bob Fredericks, "Husband Arrested After Pediatrician Wife Stabbed to Death in Shower," *New York Post*, January 20, 2016, http://nypost.com/2016/01/20/cops-question-husband-over-wifes -gruesome-murder/.
4. Dale W. Eisinger, Rocco Parascandola, and Rich Schapiro, "Blood, Sweatpants and Tears: Man Bashed into Coma in Fight Vs. Bro," *New York Daily News*, December 30, 2015, http://www.pressreader.com/usa/new-york -daily-news/20151230/281578059635319.
5. Caitlin Nolan, Rocco Parascandola, Thomas Tracy, and Corky Siemaszko, "Man Slashes Father Before Leaping to His Death from 46th Floor Upper East Side Apartment," *New York Daily News*, updated August 16, 2015, http://www.nydailynews.com/new-york/nyc-crime/man-attacked-dad -leaping-46th-floor-sources-article-1.2337622.
6. Leonard Greene, "Young Monsters: Girls, 12, 'Stabbed' Pal over Web Tale," *New York Post*, June 4, 2014, http://www.pressreader.com/usa/new-york -post/20140604/281852936625746.

7. Charles C. Mann, "Göbekli Tepe," *National Geographic*, June 2011, http://ngm.nationalgeographic.com/2011/06/gobekli-tepe/mann-text.

8. Ibid.

9. C. S. Lewis, *Mere Christianity* (New York: HarperCollins, 2009), 6.

10. J. I. Packer, *Concise Theology* (Carol Stream, IL: Tyndale House Publishers, 2011), 10.

11. Charles Wesley, "Hark! The Herald Angels Sing," composed in 1739, http://www.hymnary.org/text/hark_the_herald_angels_sing_glory_to.

12. Isaac Watts, "Joy to the World! The Lord Is Come!" composed in 1719, http://www.hymnary.org/text/joy_to_the_world_the_lord_is_come.

13. Ibid.

14. Leland Ryken, James C. Wilhoit, and Tremper Longman III, eds., *Dictionary of Biblical Imagery* (Downers Grove, IL: InterVarsity Press, 2010), 390.

15. Ibid., 391.

16. Vern Sheridan Poythress, *In the Beginning Was the Word: Language—A God-Centered Approach* (Wheaton, IL: Crossway Books, 2009), 21.

17. Carol Glatz, "Hark the Herald Angels: How Sacred Music Evangelizes, Lifts Up Hearts," Catholic News Service, December 8, 2016, http://www.catholicnews.com/services/englishnews/2016/hark-the-herald-angels-how-sacred-music-evangelizes-lifts-up-hearts.cfm.

18. Interview with Dr. Jeremy Begbie, Professor at Duke Divinity School, Duke University: March 10, 2012, New York, NY.

Chapter 9: The Song of My Heart

1. William Shakespeare, *Twelfth Night, or, What You Will* (London: Rivingtons, 1889), 10.

2. *The Unanswered Question*, Leonard Bernstein's 1973 Series of Lectures at Harvard University.

3. Michael Thaut, *Rhythm, Music, and the Brain: Scientific Foundations and Clinical Applications* (London: Routledge, 2013), viii.

4. Maureen Harris, *Music and the Young Mind: Enhancing Brain Development and Engaging Learning* (Lanham, MD: Rowman and Littlefield Education, 2009), 9.

5. E. J. Mundell, "Sorry, Kids, Piano Lessons Make You Smarter," *Forbes*, July 15, 2004, http://www.forbes.com/2004/07/15/cx_0715health.html.

6. Thomas F. Torrance, *Theological and Natural Science* (Eugene, OR: Wipf and Stock Publishers, 2005), 17.

7. Gordon L. Shaw, *Keeping Mozart in Mind*, 2nd ed. (Cambridge, MA: Elsevier Academic Press, 2004), 7–8.

8. Michio Kaku, *The Future of the Mind: The Scientific Quest to Understand, Enhance, and Empower the Mind* (New York: Anchor Books, 2015).

9. Laurence O'Donnell, "Music and the Brain," *Music Power*, 1999, http://www .cerebromente.org.br/n15/mente/musica.html.

10. Tim Neufeld, "Ancient Psalms for a State-of-the-Art Tour," ATU2.com, August 10, 2015, http://www.atu2.com/news/ancient-psalms-for-a-state-of -the-art-tour.htmlhttp://www.atu2.com/news/ancient-psalms-for-a-state-of -the-art-tour.html.

11. "The Inner Musical Cosmos," *String Theory Media*, November 19, 2008, http://www.stringtheorymedia.com/2008/11/the-inner-musical-cosmos.html.

12. C. S. Lewis, *The Lion, the Witch, and the Wardrobe* [[need rest of pub info]].

13. John D. Barrow, *The Mathematical Universe: The Orderliness of Nature Can Be Expressed Mathematically. Why?* (The Word & I, 1989), 307–11.

Chapter 10: Messiah: Lessons from a Divine Date with Destiny

1. Patrick Kavanaugh, *Spiritual Lives of the Great Composers* (Grand Rapids: Zondervan, 1996), 27.

2. Cecil B. DeMille, *The Ten Commandments*.

3. George Frideric Handel, *Messiah*.

4. Gregory Wilbur, *Glory and Honor: The Music and Artistic Legacy of Johann Sebastian Bach* (Nashville: Cumberland House Publishing, 2005), 1.

Conclusion: The Power of Three

1. "Baby Bust: The Declining U.S. Birthrate," *The Week*, December 5, 2012, http://theweek.com/articles/469808/baby-bust-declining-birthrate.

2. "Israel Honors WWII GI: Risked Life to Save US-Jewish POWs from Nazis," *New York Post*, December 3, 2015, www.pressreader.com/usa/new-york-post /20151203/281934541875083.

3. Ravi Zacharias, *The Grand Weaver: How God Shapes Us Through the Events of Our Lives* (Grand Rapids: Zondervan, 2009), 199.

Appendix: A Small Lesson in Music History and a Harmonic Analysis of the "Hallelujah Chorus"

1. Classical period in this case means the musical era of Western Europe from the mid-eighteen to early nineteenth centuries. It does not mean the general name for the style of music.

2. Rita Steblin, trans., "Affective Key Characteristics," *A History of Key Characteristics in the 18th and Early 19th Centuries*, UMI Research Press, 1983, http://www.wmich.edu/mus-theo/courses/keys.html.

Printed in the USA
CPSIA information can be obtained
at www.ICGtesting.com
JSHW03225627O524
63867JS00017B/477

9 781400 341641